Stars of A&E's **Flipping Vegas**

# SCOTT & AMIE YANCEY

# *FLIPPING* YOUR WAY

## TO **REAL ESTATE PROFITS**

**PLUS:** *Use Our Top* ***Rebounding-Market Strategies*** *for Long-Term Success!*

**FLIPPING YOUR WAY TO REAL ESTATE PROFITS**
Published by: Yancey LLC
Copyright © 2014

Printed in the United States of America
First Printing Novemeber of 2014

Neither the author nor Yancey LLC, in any way make any warranty, guaranty or representation, expressed or implied, as to the potential volume, profits, or success of any activity or undertaking described herein.

All information related to the potential to earn money or realize a profit from any activity described herein was recieved from third parties and was not created or verified by the author or Yancey LLC, or any agent of either of them.

Neither the author nor Yancey LLC, in any way warrant or confirm the accuracy of any information provided herein.

The reader should conduct an independent investigation into the information contained herein before taking any action.

The success or failure of any undertaking described herein or based on the information provided herein may involve financial risks solely dependent upon the reader's own ability and efforts, changes in technology or shifts in market realities.

Finally nothing contained herein should be construed as legal advice.

Regulations vary from state to state, and change from time to time.

Consult your own independent legal counsel as to the legality of any undertaking before taking action based on information contained herein.

# Contents

## Introduction

Hi, I'm Scott Yancey, and my hit TV show "Flipping Vegas" on the A&E television network is all about fix & flip real estate investing. It's been a fun adventure, and I do love to fix up homes and resell them for short-term profits. But, there's so much more in the way of opportunity in real estate investment, and this book is all about delivering on the promise of profits in all real estate investment strategies in every market cycle.

If fix & flip turns out to be your preferred real estate investment strategy, that's great. But, people and their goals are diverse, and I don't want anyone to turn away from the awesome opportunities in real estate simply because they're not into one popular strategy or niche.

This book takes you through seven profitable real estate investment niche strategies, and delivers what you need to know to take off from the starting line and see profits right away. I hope that every reader sees at least a couple of immediate opportunities for their new business and that they use the tools I'm introducing here to improve their finances and lives.

### The Foundation

I don't just jump into specific strategies, as this isn't the best approach for success. There is a foundation to build for support and sound business practices. You're starting a new business, and you'll need to do some planning and self-assessment to see how to approach what you'll learn in this book.

We go through some exercises to understand your goals, risk tolerance, and available resources. There will be one or more investment niche strategies in this book that will work for everyone. However, it's important to understand what we want, as well as the resources in time, knowledge and finances we have to invest in our new business. You'll get these questions out of the way in the first few chapters, and you'll move forward with a much clearer plan for success.

## *Tools and Resources*

Then we spend a few chapters on the tools and resources you need to create and grow your business. These include investment calculations for buying and selling, research tools to become a local real estate market expert, business tools, and home value calculation.

We take an in-depth look at outsourcing properly, the selection of vendors and support businesses, and building a team focused not only on their profits, but your success and continued business as well. You can stay in control, and you should. But, it's your business, and we want to get you started right in accessing expertise and services to grow your business and free up your time for other things.

Before I take you through each of the investment niche strategies, I help you to identify and quantify the ways in which you bring value to the table for each niche. You can only be successful if your customers see and understand the value you bring to the table. I show you how to build a buyer list of customers, as well as how to market for motivated sellers for product. We get the basics of foreclosures and short sales under your belt as well.

There is a very important chapter about funding your deals. I give you specific funding resources, including some you may have never considered, but they're working for investors every day. It's important to know that the availability of money is not an issue that should limit your desire to jump into any of the strategies you will learn about in this book.

## *Niche Strategies and How to Make them Work for You*

With all of this foundation material in front, you're ready to move through the strategies you can use in your business. One or more of them should work for you right away, and you could end up doing most of them in the long run through to your retirement. If you're close to or in retirement, you'll find strategies here perfect for cash flow and an improved lifestyle. We go through these niche strategies in detail:

- Bird Dogging
- Wholesaling – Two Approaches

- Fix & Flip
- Rental Property Investing
- Leases and Sandwich Leases
- Mortgage Notes Investing
- Tax Lien Investing

*You can see that there are many ways to profit in real estate, and one or more of them will work for you right now. Everything you need to get started is in this book. Let's get down to business!*

### Chapter 1

## *You Aren't Born with a Real Estate Gene*

*"To succeed in life you need two things: ignorance and confidence."*
*– Mark Twain*

I like the Mark Twain quote because too many of us fear trying something new; we think we don't know enough and may fail before we get up to speed. Strangely enough, you're going to succeed as a real estate investor in good part because of ignorance:

- You don't know about the bad habits that bring failure.
- You are a clean slate, and this book will fill your slate with the right stuff for success.

If you've already dabbled in real estate investing without success, get back to being ignorant and we'll take you from novice to expert in these pages. As you read and study, you'll build that other thing Mark Twain says you need: confidence.

## My confidence head start came from my grandfather.

I got a little bit of a head start on building confidence in real estate as a profitable business thanks to my grandfather. Growing up in North Hollywood, my parents weren't wealthy. We got by, though. When I was nine years old, my parents divorced and my mother, brother, and I moved in with my grandparents.

My grandfather was a real estate agent, doing well enough to appear rich to me. He lived in a nice home in Studio City and owned several Cadillacs. He took me under his real estate wing and I rode around with him to property showings and Open Houses in a Cadillac convertible with the top down.

The important thing about this story is that I didn't know or think anything about real estate until I was exposed to it by my grandfather. It doesn't matter how old you are or whether you've ever bought or sold a home. You're going to get the exposure you need here, and you're going to have the tools and knowledge you need when you finish this book to start a profitable real estate investment business.

## You don't learn by watching – you learn by doing.

With the real estate seed sown by my grandfather, I got my second exposure to the business in college. I took a part-time job with real estate partners Walt Plumb and Ron Ferrin. Their influence and the experience I gained working with them has lasted a lifetime. I talk to them frequently, and we still do deals together.

I started as a runner with Walt, but he took me under his wing and taught me a lot about real estate and development. You learn by doing, and Walt tossed me into the deep end of the real estate pool right away. He owned a 40 unit apartment complex, but wanted to sell them off as a condo project. He didn't tell me how to do it; he just said that he wanted me to turn them into condominiums and sell them off.

This was my first introduction to working with people who have money but are either unwilling or unable to take on some investment activities. They'll gladly turn them over to you if they have faith in your abilities and your desire to succeed as much for them as for yourself.

That condo project was my first real solo experience, and it was sink or swim on my own. I worked with local government, planning and zoning, and building inspectors to complete the transition from apartments to condos. My first month I banked $30,000 in commissions on sales. While you do learn a lot from watching others, you can also absorb and profit from just jumping in and doing something. Throughout this book, I'm going to be encouraging you to do something in every chapter.

Later in the book we'll talk about bird-dogging as both a profit center and a learning experience. After the condo deal, I was bird-dogging for Walt and Ron in Utah ski resort development. The profits in these projects came from locating multiple pieces of property and combining them into a larger and more valuable tract for development.

Once we had a tract ready for development, I moved into working with the local government as well as building, planning, and zoning agencies to get the subdivisions approved. We often would get approval to turn 100 acre properties into 500 or more lots for development. I wasn't reading about it and dreaming … I was hip deep in getting it done.

In my 20s, I was an employee but definitely a working partner in the development process with Walt and Ron. I got my real estate license to leverage it into more value to the company. During this time I sold more than 800 lots to one developer in a dozen subdivisions.

My deal with this developer/builder was to use my real estate broker's license to market the homes being built. With a broker's license I could hire real estate sales people. I did that, hired staff, and worked with title companies and other vendors and real estate service providers. From all of these activities, I learned the real estate business from front to back.

We sold more than 200 homes in nine months. I couldn't get to the bank in Park City fast enough, even though I was driving a Hummer and a Land Rover. The "doing it" thing works both ways

though. It was great driving new cars and raking in the money …
until the market took a downward turn. I took a hit on some deals,
decided the good times there were done for a while, and so I moved
to Las Vegas, Nevada.

## Don't be locally limited.

I didn't abandon Utah entirely. I started doing some retail de-
partment store development in Provo, as well as in Las Vegas and
Tempe, AZ. It was going OK, and I was learning all along the way.
During this time I met Jon Quitiquit, an old land partner of Walt's.
He travelled doing land deals, and every time he passed through
town he was driving something newer and better.

Jon was always inviting me to partner on deals and giving me a
hard time for being slow to jump in. He liked to say, "When you're
tired of folding sweaters, you should start making millions with
me." Every time he came through with a different car, it seemed to
be more expensive than the one before, so I paid attention.

In 2005 we met with others, including Guy Tomlinson, and
formed a partnership to do land deals in California. I'm sure you'll
agree that when you're travelling from another state to do land
deals, you really have to be driving a fast car. It was a prudent business , then, that we buy four Porsche Cayenne Turbos! Or, at least
we convinced ourselves that it was a business decision. I put more
than 50k miles on mine that first year of doing deals.

## Success takes hard work and dedication.

I said you learn by doing, and that you can get rich investing
in real estate. I didn't say that it would fall into your lap. In putting
those 50,000 miles on the Porsche that year, I travelled from one
end of California to the other without even doing one deal. I was
dead tired all the time, and only got rest when I became sick and
had to stay in bed for a couple of days.

Maybe it was the rest, some good luck, or just the fact that my
time had come, but I made a deal. I'd been working with some
farmers for six months trying to put together a land deal, buying

from them and selling to a developer/builder. I finally got the farmers to agree to sell and found a builder who wanted to build out a subdivision. He offered me $40,000 more per acre than I was paying for the land. I had finally put together a deal, and it netted me a whopping $2.3 million!

### When it works, do it again … better.

This deal gave me the confidence and a plan that became a formula for success. I started by talking to builders, asking them where they wanted land for building. I also checked out where development was already going on. I wasn't an expert at all things real estate, so I also consulted with title companies, engineers, and planning departments to target the best areas for development.

Once I decided where I wanted to do deals, I would contact farmers and large tract owners in those areas. Building relationships and keeping a discussion going about selling, I would just wear them down until they agreed to sell. It was a good system that I knew would generate profits.

Using this system, I did another dozen or so deals over a couple of years. I sold more than a thousand lots, and just kept doing it over and over as long as it kept working. Two things happen when you do this: 1) you learn and get better with each deal, and 2) you make a whole lot of money.

### When it works, enjoy the success.

My wife was enthusiastic and supportive of my success, telling me that I should enjoy it. One night as she was falling off to sleep, I swear she gave me the go-ahead to buy myself a Porsche as a reward for my success. At least that's the way I remember it. When I showed her the car I bought for a six figure price, she couldn't remember authorizing a deal of that size, but it was done, so I took her for a ride and nice dinner.

Cars are my thing, and that was the first of many. We don't live to work; we work to live, and success makes living more fun.

## When it's over, admit it and move on.

Suddenly it was like the downhill run was over, and my business was struggling to climb a steep grade. It no longer was deal after deal with competing builder offers. It became calls for discounts, extensions, and total bailouts from deals. People were having problems selling their homes and developments, so they backed up to us as their suppliers wanting concessions. At a certain point, there were no more concessions available at a profit. Though we didn't lose money, the days of big deals were winding down.

My wife and I were in transition mode, discussing what to do and where to do it. We decided to sell our home, and the plan was to move down to Cabo San Lucas and enjoy our beach home there. We put our home up for sale, got an instant offer that was over asking price, and the buyers bought everything in it too!

### Don't be too quick … my almost biggest mistake.

We had sold our home, but we couldn't just get on the road south. There were a few deals to wrap up, so we were taking care of those before leaving. We leased an empty house, threw in some lawn furniture, and were just waiting out the move.

It was during this time that we were hanging out a lot at coffee shops because their furniture was more comfortable than ours. Purely by chance one day, I overheard a conversation at the next table. You know how you can "kind of" hear what people are saying, but you're not really that interested so it kind of just washes over and past you.

That's what I was doing until I heard someone say, *"I can buy a home in Las Vegas right now for $36,000 to $50,000 and rent it out for $900/month."* Suddenly the conversation went from washing past me to the center of my attention. All of those things my grand-father and Walt had told me about opportunities in real estate were suddenly front and center.

I realized that there are so many more ways to make money in this business than just my past focus on major land deals. I also re-alized that there was no way that I was going to hang out on a beach with a margarita while others were raking in real estate profits.

I called a real estate agent friend and asked her if the cheap houses thing and good rents were real. She did a quick search of the MLS and told me that there were at least 75 cheap homes for sale that would cash flow for great rental profits. That's all I needed to hear, so I told her to make a $36,000 purchase offer on every one of them!

Over the next few months I averaged getting one of these homes under contract each week. It was goodbye Cabo and hello Vegas. I had almost made the biggest mistake of my life. I was assuming that when my previous boom business was over that it was time to get out of the business altogether. That overheard coffee shop conversation made me dig into my past and realize that there is opportunity in every market cycle.

### The worst of times are the best of times for some.

The real estate and mortgage crash that began in 2007 had taken the Las Vegas real estate market from a major boom to a dramatic bust. Homes were selling for a fifth of their previous market value, and there were a lot of them. I began to make offers and buy at discounts up to and over 75% of pre-bust market value!

The people who lost their homes to foreclosure weren't necessarily out of work or leaving the area either. Many simply got caught with toxic mortgage products, like Adjustable Rate Mortgages, that resulted in sudden jumps in their rates and payments. They couldn't afford to keep that home, but they still needed somewhere to live. They became renters, and they could afford to pay rents that created a good cash flow for me because I could buy foreclosed homes at such deep discounts.

All I did was move from deal-by-deal, "bank the profits investing" to a longer term approach to creating wealth. Sure, I could have been fishing and soaking up the sun, but that would have become boring pretty quickly. It's a lesson in recognizing that there is always a profit opportunity no matter how the markets are moving : up, down, or sideways. I'm going to show you how to profit from real estate.

### So, you want to follow me around with a TV camera?

I was happily buying cheap houses, bringing them up to rentable condition, filling them with tenants, and taking the rent profits to the bank every month. Remember that I grew up around the TV and movie business in California, and one day I got a phone call from a friend in the business. He was pushing me hard to do a "reality" TV show about what I do every day.

After more phone calls, I decided to put a toe into the water. My plan was to do a kind of short commercial, a "sizzle reel," of a few minutes about what I do every day in real estate. We started the day intending to get a few minutes of edited film, but it ended up being a solid, interesting 45 minutes. Since the average hour long TV show is around 43 minutes of content without commercials, we had an episode.

For the serious real estate investor, it's a really big drag to have to worry about microphone placement, audio and video quality, and constant interruptions to get you to do things over again. We got it done, though, and agreed that if anything came from the pilot it would be nice. But, we also agreed that if it bombed we'd be just as happy to continue our real estate activities and going to the bank.

To our surprise, it was a hit, and we were picked up by A&E network for a series. We've got several seasons under our belt now, and it's been fun and educational experience.

### Helping investors one email at a time … OR

The success of *Flipping Vegas* has been very gratifying, and it also made us a household fixture for people who want to improve their lives and futures investing in real estate. We began to get hundreds of emails every day, many wanting advice and asking questions.

We also began to do some personal appearances and seminars to instruct others in the basics of real estate investing, especially about the long-term wealth creation with rental property investing. Sure, we're still flipping too, but it's more intensive an activity, and some investors prefer other wealth strategies. You can only answer so many emails and talk to so many people personally. It wasn't helping enough people to suit me.

This brings me to what this book and my previous book Go Time are all about. This book expands on the many ways to profit in real estate, and this applies to you, no matter what your current job or financial situation. It doesn't matter what you know, how much money you have, or whether you have any experience in real estate or not.

It's great if you've bought and sold a few personal homes, but that's the retail market, buying and selling on features and emotions. In this business, you may start out faster if you take Mark

Twain's quote at the start of the chapter to heart. You need both ignorance and confidence to be successful.

This book will help you launch a profitable real estate investing business:

- Whether you have a lot of cash to invest or not.
- Even if you've never bought or sold a home.
- Whether or not you have ever invested in the stock market.

This book is how I can help thousands of people to create wealth in real estate without sending tens of thousands of emails. You don't have to wait for a response, and you don't have to find a seminar to attend. You just need to read and take action.

---

### Perspective & Progress

Take a look at your local real estate market, both today and over the past few years. Your goal at the end of this chapter is to recognize the opportunities that have been there all through the ups and downs in the market, especially since the peak in 2006.

No matter how bad it may have gotten or how many foreclosure signs you saw, almost all of those homes are still sitting there, and they're not empty. How many were sold to investors and are occupied by happy tenants? What changes have come over the past seven years in your real estate market? Who has been making the money?

Understanding the changing opportunities that were there all along and who took advantage of those opportunities will help you begin to move on that second thing Mark Twain says you need: confidence.

*Chapter 2*

---

# *Stocks & Bonds Can Crash & Burn-*
# *Real Estate is Insurance*

*"Risk is what's left over when you think you've thought of everything."*
*– Carl Richards*

For most of us, the amount of time we spend thinking about investing and retirement is related to our age. The younger we are, the less we tend to think about it and the less we do about it. As we age, we think much more about what we'll do to fund our lifestyle after we stop working at our full-time career.

Few of us, except those of us already collecting it, believe we can or should rely on Social Security. So our thoughts turn to investments and how to grow a nest egg for the future. The vast majority of the American public is invested in stocks and bonds in one way or another.

Even if you have an employer-sponsored retirement plan, it's almost certain that the assets in that plan are dominated by stocks and bonds. There's nothing wrong with that since we need to have some of our invested money in the stock market and, as we get closer to retirement, the bond market.

It's interesting how investment advisors will chant the mantra "diversify, diversify…diversify," yet keep your entire future tied up in just two asset classes. Sure, they put your money into different industries and split it up among the stock shares of many companies, but it's still just stocks and/or bonds.

They'll also have you in some income-producing bonds, as the consensus is that they're a lot safer than stocks. The trade-off is that the return on bonds is usually much lower than stocks as a whole. "Generally safer" is a relative term, though. The bondholders in General Motors were quite upset when their interests were subordinated to those of the unions, and they lost a lot of money.

Mutual funds allow even greater diversification with lower dollar investments. This allows you to start younger, invest small amounts regularly, and hopefully grow your portfolio value over time. You rely on experts to choose the stocks and bonds in the funds based on the stated goals of the fund. But, they're still just a basket of stocks or bonds, carrying the risks and disadvantages that go with those asset classes.

There are advantages and disadvantages with every asset class, but there can be dramatic differences in their relative value over the long haul. Let's take a quick look at stocks, bonds, mutual funds, and real estate in order to get an overview.

## Stocks – Advantages

- You can choose well-established companies with long histories of profits.
- Diversification among business types and companies is easy. You can buy stocks in financial, manufacturing, technology, and other company groups.
- There are choices between growth stocks and those that are

more oriented to paying dividends.

- Stocks are liquid investments, easily bought and sold and with low commission costs of trading.
- History shows that over the very long haul, stocks have appreciated in value.

## Stocks – Disadvantages

- Your future is in the hands of the management of the companies in which you invest. Good decisions are great for you, while bad ones can be disastrous.
- That "very long haul" appreciation advantage can never materialize for you if for some reason you have a shorter time span or must take out funds for other purposes. See the chart below for the stock market crashes of the past.
- Because brokerages make money on trading commissions, there is a lot of encouragement to trade rather than hold. This can definitely work against your long-term interests.
- Most stocks carry inflation risk. Rising prices eat away at your return. In other words, if you're getting a 6% per year return on your stocks but inflation is 4%, you've dropped by two-thirds.

As you can see, how well you do in the stock market can be very different depending on when you enter and when you exit an investment.

## Bonds – Advantages

Bonds are loans to corporations or the government secured by the assets of the corporation or the "good faith and credit" of the government. You loan them money, and they guarantee you a defined rate of return over a specified period of time.

In other words, you can buy a 10 year bond that pays x% interest and matures in 10 years. You receive regular monthly or quarterly interest payments, and at the end of the 10 years, you get all of your principal back (or you're supposed to).

- Bonds are normally more secure than stocks.
- You know the return you're going to receive on your investment.
- You can buy and sell bonds like you can stocks.
- Older individuals and retirees can enjoy a definite monthly income they can count on to pay the bills.

## Bonds – Disadvantages

- They aren't always secure, as companies can and do go bankrupt.
- When a company goes under, bondholders have a place near the front of the line of creditors, but there is often not enough in assets at sale to pay them back.
- Bonds carry both inflation and interest rate risk. Inflation eats away at those interest payments. If interest rates rise after you buy a bond and you need or want to sell it, its value will be less because investors would rather buy a new bond at the current higher interest rate.

## Mutual Funds – Advantages

- With a basket of stocks or bonds, you are automatically somewhat diversified, which should reduce risk of industry or individual company troubles.
- Mutual funds with experienced and successful managers can realize higher returns than the market as a whole be-

cause the managers are picking the right stocks and buying and selling at the right times.

- Mutual funds can specialize in industries, such as a technology fund only investing in stocks or bonds of companies like *Apple*, *Microsoft*, or *Google*. This concentrates knowledge and research, hopefully making investment decisions more accurate.
- You can buy into them with much smaller sums of money, without needing to buy a minimum number of a company's shares.
- Many of them will allow you to set up monthly investments on an automatic plan out of your bank account. You can "set it and forget it."

## Mutual Funds – Disadvantages

- That reliance on the skill of the managers can turn on you if they're calling the market or their niche wrong.
- Funds can get too big to be effective. Once a fund gets too large, it's more difficult to invest the amount of money available, as buying into a company too heavily creates share cost increases.
- Mutual funds are like large ships, not small fast boats of individual company shares. It takes a while to turn a large ship, and sometimes it's too long for market conditions.
- All of the interest rate and inflation negative influences apply to a basket of stocks or bonds, just like the individual assets themselves. Mutual funds carry market, interest, and inflation risks across their portfolios.

## Real Estate – Advantages

Before we list them, let's be sure that we understand that there are many different ways to make money in real estate. Some are more risky than others, and some are much more lucrative because of increased risk. This is a general discussion of these investments as a group:

- Real estate is a finite asset. A company can issue more shares of stock, or it can bring a new bond issue to market to borrow more money. Doing either dilutes the value of shares or bonds as a whole because the company is still the same size with the same financials. There won't be any more land created unless we start settling other planets.
- Demand for real estate is directly related to population, and the world's population is continuously growing.
- Real estate is insurable. You can insure your rental home against casualty losses, while your company stocks can go to zero value overnight, and there's no insurance for that.
- Historically, real estate has appreciated in value. The crash in 2007 wiped out a huge amount of real estate wealth, but seven years later many areas were back to the home price levels in 2006.
- Interest rate risk isn't as much of a problem for real estate. It's true that selling is more difficult if rates are high, but a rental property is still generating the same rent, and the property is still appreciating in value.
- Inflation is also less of a problem with real estate; in fact it can help with values and rents. As prices for labor and materials rise, it becomes more expensive to build new homes, so they rise in price. This causes existing home values to rise as well. When it's more expensive to buy, people move to rentals, so rents may go up.
- There are tax advantages enjoyed by real estate investors that aren't available to investors in stocks and bonds. We'll get specific later, but there are capital gains deferrals and depreciation deductions that make real estate very attractive for tax avoidance or deferral.

## Real Estate – Disadvantages

- You can't buy and sell it with a phone call to a broker. It's not as liquid as stocks and bonds. Of course, if you're a day trader type, you won't be messing with real estate anyway.
- Real estate is more expensive to buy and sell due to com-

missions and closing costs.

- There are costs to hold real estate, including property taxes, repairs, and insurance. However, adjusting rents to cover those with a profit is what investing is all about.

## Risk and Reward

There is definitely a trade-off between risk and reward. Playing it safe with investing is a strategy, but it will cost you a lot over the course of your investing life. Real estate offers an intelligent balance between risk and reward. Double-digit returns are possible with much less risk than lower overall returns with stocks and bonds.

---

### Perspective & Progress

Take some time to think about your tolerance for risk. Balance that with your desire to build a successful real estate investment business with returns well above those of the average investor in stocks and bonds.

It doesn't have to be an either-or decision. Diversification is a good thing, so it's more of a weighing of proportions. How much of your focus and what proportion of your investable assets will be committed to each asset class?

The good thing about real estate investment is that you can start with little or no cash of your own. In fact, some investors specialize in low cash niche strategies as their entire investment business plan.

---

### Chapter 3

## Start With You – Where You Are

*"Ability is what you're capable of doing. Motivation determines what you do. Attitude determines how well you do it." – Lou Holtz*

### You Can Do This!

In this chapter we're going to work on assessing your abilities, attitude, strengths, weaknesses, financial situation, and desires. We're not doing it to see if you can do this or be a successful real estate investor, because you can. We're doing it to help you set attainable goals and start with the best investment strategy for success. This doesn't limit you to that starting strategy. It just makes sure that you start with an attainable goal. You'll make a profit, and it's off to the races from there.

## Your Financial Situation

You're going to balance your current financial situation and resources with your tolerance for risk, abilities, and preferences for different investment activities. Some of the strategies in this book require little or no cash out of pocket, and many investors start with those. Others require an upfront investment, and you may have the money to start with those.

### *Your Tolerance for Risk*

This isn't as important in real estate investment as it is in stocks, bonds, options, and commodities investment. That's because there is less risk in real estate, and the risk that exists is more controllable in real estate investing. However, you still want to have an idea of how you'll react to a project that breaks even or loses money.

Your risk tolerance will be less about whether or not you use some of these strategies and more about how you go about using them. An example: If you are risk averse, you'll want to be as certain as possible that you have a buyer lined up before executing an assignment contract to buy a home. This may take the form of spending a lot more time building your buyer list before you take on a deal. It may mean you'll work harder to cut the amount of earnest money necessary for the deal so you'll risk less if the buyer side doesn't happen.

You shouldn't think about your tolerance for risk in relation to your available cash, but at first it may be important. If you only have a few hundred dollars, that first deal can be critical if you don't have the money to do another assignment with earnest money. But, if you're cash poor, you may want to do some bird-dogging first to build up the cash you have available to grow your business.

Right now just take the time to think about how you felt or acted if and when you lost money on investments in the past. Even if you were just buying and selling used household stuff on *eBay* or *Craigslist*, how did you react when it didn't work out the way you wanted? Keep this in mind when you're deciding on which strategies to start with.

### Cash Available for Real Estate Investing

I would much rather you start out with no-cash strategies in this book than risk cash you need for other things or for emergencies. We all need a cash reserve for emergencies, from car repairs to medical stuff. Don't dip into your emergency cash for real estate investment.

We should all have a cushion to pay bills if we have an income interruption. If you don't, think about putting that back before you tie up cash in real estate investment. Estimates of what you need vary, but it's probably minimal to have three or four months of bill coverage cash for income emergencies.

In a later chapter I'll give you some resources and specific information on funding your deals. Right now, just create a quick spreadsheet or listing of funds you may have available for real estate:

- Checking accounts
- Savings accounts
- Certificates of deposit
- Investment accounts
- Retirement accounts
- Home equity
- Other property equity

Don't worry right now about how you may be able to tap this money, as we'll deal with that in the chapter about funding your deals. For now, just get a good picture of what you have for funds, how much of it is crucial to your lifestyle or retirement, and how much may be available for real estate investment.

### How Much Time is Available?

Just like in our money discussion, this isn't about limiting what you can do or where you start in real estate investment. We want to take a realistic look at the time you have to commit to your new business, including an exercise you can do that almost always results in freeing up time you don't realize you have.

Start with the most important thing in your life: your family. Involving your family in your dream of successful real estate investment is a good thing, but you don't want to require sacrifices on their part or reduce your family time unnecessarily. But letting them in on your dream will help them understand the changes you'll be making in your life and how you will use your time.

There may be some family activities that you can modify to free up some time. Take a look at your daily routines to see if there is any duplication of effort, or if trading off activities with your significant other can add a little time to the business side of the ledger. One big factor we've found in family time management is the home to-dos and maintenance tasks. I know that I can have a tendency to jump on small do-it-myself stuff when the need arises.

I pull out the tools and tighten a cabinet pull or adjust a doorknob. I realized that setting up a specific time and day of the week to do all of the little things at once freed up an hour or so. Pulling out those tools only once is more efficient.

### Hobbies and Fun Time

Setting your sights on a successful and profitable real estate business shouldn't make your life one of constant work. You still want to enjoy your hobbies and fun with the family. But sacrificing some of your "messing around" time in the workshop or dropping every other fishing trip for a while might be a profitable decision.

Do you have a coffee house habit that absorbs an hour or more every week? Giving it up isn't necessary, but perhaps cutting the time or frequency of your visits will free up time. Do you go out to lunch at work? If you brought your lunch, would it give you some time to do some of the tasks necessary for success in real estate investment? Don't forget, though, to factor in the time to prepare that lunch.

### Plain Old Wasted or Idle Time

This may be time you don't even recognize right now, even if you think about it. To get to the root of your time efficiency, do a time analysis exercise like the efficiency experts do it. In a notepad or on your smart phone, start noting down what you do all day every day and how long you do it. Check out the app stores for time journal apps for your smart phone to make this faster and easier. Do it for at least a week, because you have different activities on the days you don't work. Two weeks is better.

- Are you doing repetitive things that could be combined to save time?

- What do you find that's repetitive that could be completely avoided?

- Will changing the days or times when you do a repetitive thing save time overall?

- Even changing travel routes to and from work or regularly scheduled activities could be wasting time.

Some people are amazed after this exercise at the time they are wasting on a regular basis. You'll have the time for a real estate investment business, but freeing up more time will increase your profits and ultimate success.

### *Your Talents and Abilities*

**Math:** Are you a financial wizard or do you have a problem balancing your checkbook? Some people don't even bother to try it. Does this mean you can't invest in real estate? Absolutely not! Sure, there's some math involved if you really want to do it right and maximize profits.

But it's easy math, and we're going to give you the calculations in this book, as well as access to a spreadsheet so that you simply enter the numbers you gather and your rental property financial analysis appears right in front of your eyes with no math on your part! Don't let an aversion to math slow you down a bit.

**Handy Person:** Do you do carpentry, repair cabinets and doors, change fuses and breakers, and take care of minor plumbing repairs around the house? Or do you have a handy person or repair company on speed dial? It doesn't matter.

Actually, when we talk about fix & flip, you'll quickly see that you limit your success and profits if you try to do it all yourself. Why do one deal, work hard all day on the fix-it stuff, then go home tired and have to do the accounting? All you have to do is leverage your business by hiring the right people for each job, and we'll show you just how to do that.

If you do have some experience and abilities related to the trades, it's definitely a plus when you're evaluating the work of the people you hire. But you can learn enough to know when an electrician is running wiring efficiently or when routing it the long way is costing you money.

### Attitude – Yours and Everyone Else's

Sure, you want to succeed and improve your financial situation and secure your retirement. That's a given. But, since we're assessing our abilities, let's talk about our attitude and the attitude of others around us, because attitudes can make you rich or destroy your dream … if you let them.

First, you're reading this, so you must be looking forward to profiting from a successful real estate investment business. You're motivated to change your financial situation and improve your life. I don't think that a lot of hype about "You can to this and become rich!" is going to motivate you any more effectively.

My idea of motivation is seeing that you can do something because you're exposed to the knowledge, tools, and resources to get it done well. When you realize that you're learning the right way and getting the best tools and resources for success, you'll be even more motivated.

**The Negative Side:** The discussion here is crucial, simply because failure to launch or failure to succeed in real estate investing is often rooted in you being influenced by the negative attitudes of others. You'll want to let your family, friends and co-workers know about your real estate investment business and plans. It's just good business, as some of them can probably refer you some business right away. But watch out for and totally ignore:

- Your father's story about Uncle Roy buying a rental house years ago and taking a financial beating because of bad tenants, damage, and non-payment of rent. Negativity from family members is usually just concern for your welfare, so take it in the spirit in which it's offered.

- Your best friend's fear of financial calamity because they have zero risk tolerance and low self-esteem. They are immediately telling you about the horrors of losing your savings and the big housing crash of 2007.

- Or, and we all know them, the people who don't have the drive or initiative to improve their lives so they're jealous when you do. They are full of negativity that they are only too willing to share.

These negative people are really a blessing in disguise. They're never going to be competition. Once you're successful, you may be approached with requests to get involved. We'll talk about this later when we get to the chapter on funding. Stay positive, ignore negativity, learn the success tutorials in this book, and you'll be just fine … more than fine!

---

### Perspective & Progress

This chapter is probably one of the most important when we think of "perspective." Your expectations for business success and profits in real estate will at this point be based on a foundation of attitude and a belief that you will succeed.

Do the exercises in this chapter, think about any extra time you have or can free up, understand your financial situation and abilities, and be realistic as to your tolerance for risk. This will be your perspective on success going forward, and it will make learning the tools fun and easy.

As for progress, you've set the stage for moving through the nuts and bolts of real estate investment in the rest of the book. You know what you want, what you have to work with, and now you simply need to learn what you need to do to get there.

---

### Chapter 4

## *Start With You – Where You Want to Be & Build Your Plan*

*"One important key to success is self-confidence. An important key to self-confidence is preparation." – Arthur Ashe*

If you're starting a business and you want to get a small business loan, you're going to have to jump through some hoops at the bank or with the Small Business Administration. The biggest is the submission of a comprehensive business plan outlining the business, products/services, and a plan for starting, managing and marketing the business. They'll want to know precisely how you plan on making the business profitable.

This chapter is a little like a business plan tutorial, but not nearly as formal. How do you plan on achieving your real estate investment business goals if you don't define them, give them substance, and set down a plan to reach your objective? You may pull it off without a written set of major and interim goals, but you'd be the exception rather than the rule.

### Goals Aren't Dreams – They're Mandatory Objectives

Get out a pad or your computer, because it's time to get serious about setting goals that you'll work through to your ultimate goal of a successful and profitable real estate investment business. It's important to know now that this is just the first version of your goals and plan. As you go through this book, you'll learn more about real estate investment, and you'll be adding to and changing this first version. It's a work in progress.

I like the **SMART** approach to goal setting, meaning that goals should be:

- Specific
- Measurable
- Achievable
- Realistic
- Timely

Using the SMART approach, you will create goals that contribute to your success, and you'll get them done.

### SPECIFIC

"I want to be rich by the time I'm 40 years old" is not specific. Though you may get to 40 and have a lot of money in the bank, just what is "rich" to you? Perhaps a better way to set a long-term goal like this one would be "I want to have 10 rental properties generating positive cash flow by the time I'm 40 years old." The number 10 is specific.

## *MEASURABLE*

Our specific goal is an example, as we can measure our progress toward getting it done. With each new rental property we place in service, we're measuring progress. Setting a goal to add a specific number of new buyers to your buyer list every six months is another example. You can count new buyers as they're added and measure progress as you go.

## *ACHIEVABLE*

Setting goals you can't reasonably attain is discouraging and won't help you to succeed. In our examples so far, setting a goal to own 100 rental homes by the age of 40 when you're 35 would be an example. More power to you if you can do it, but it's doubtful unless you own a bank.

Set goals that you expect to reasonably achieve. It's OK to set them low at first because you don't have any past performance to go by. In our buyer list example, you may set a goal to add one or two new investor buyers each month to your list. If you find that you're doing better than that every month, you can ratchet up your goal to push yourself a little. Constantly achieving your goals builds confidence.

## *REALISTIC*

This is closely related to Achievable. If you set goals that can't be accomplished, you're just going to be discouraged. Also, realistic could apply to setting goals that aren't really going to be helpful in building your business. Setting a goal to read every *New York Times* bestseller book within a week of when it reaches that list may be something you enjoy personally, but it's unlikely to be important to your success in real estate investment. Of course, this book is a major exception!

## *TIMELY*

In one way this is related to Achievable, as setting too tight of a timeline for achieving a goal will guarantee that you won't be successful on time. But there's also a market factor in real estate investment goal setting. Timely can also relate to the current market conditions. There's a successful real estate investing strategy for every market, up, down, or sideways. But using a rising market strategy in a falling market wouldn't be wise.

## Long-Term & Interim Goal Setting

Your first goals should be set looking into the future. Our 10 rentals by age 40 goal is an example, though the age can change based on your current age. Set long-term goals first. You may not really have a firm idea of specific numbers, so starting that goal something like "Having enough rental properties to pay my bills with cash flow by 45 years old" could be an approach. You don't really know what your bills will be by then, but it's a goal that helps you get started. You can change it at any time, including putting down specific numbers as you gain experience and start doing deals.

Once you have long-term goals defined, break them down into smaller goals with closer timelines. In our rental properties example, you could set a goal to have the first property in service within a year, or whatever time frame seems right for you. Then you can set interim goals to reach that one year goal:

- Marketing for motivated sellers in place this month.
- Locate, view, and value at least 10 foreclosure properties each month.
- Develop a rental market analysis within 30 days.
- Make an offer on one property each month until a deal is made.

You're getting the idea. Business goals become a business plan with real benchmarks for success. Unless you've done a lot of goal setting and planning in the past, you'll stumble around a bit doing this, but it's a work in progress. You should expect to change goals and timelines as you learn more and gain experience in the real world marketplace.

Part of the process is to set up a system of monitoring and measuring your progress. You don't want to bump into goal deadlines, suddenly realizing that you've missed the mark because you weren't watching. Review your interim goals daily if they're on a short timetable. It's better to adjust the timeline and attain your goal than to suddenly find you've missed it because you weren't watching and measuring your progress.

---

### Perspective & Progress

If you're a seat-of-the-pants type personality, you may want to skip this goal-setting exercise. I don't recommend that, but you can pare it down to a set of statements or bullet points of what you want to accomplish this week, next week, and then next month.

I think it's better if those bullet points are related to some attainable longer-term goal, but the key is to set down some type of plan now, and to start working on it. As you move through this book, you'll be adding to and modifying your goals based on what you're learning and the strategies you decide to use.

There's no doubt that one of your early goals if you're new to this is to learn as much as possible about your local real estate market. There's a chapter coming up on this subject, but the next chapter will help you to gather, file, and retrieve that knowledge when you need it.

---

### Chapter 5

# *The Swiss Army Knife for Your Real Estate Investment Business*

*"Getting information off the Internet is like taking a drink from a fire hydrant." – Mitchell Kapor*

I like that quote about the Internet and fire hydrant because it illustrates that all of the information available causes us to suffer from information overload. Just having access to billions of online pages isn't of any help if we're not increasing our real estate investing knowledge or we can't find what we need when we need it. It's not just the Web, either. Successful real estate investors are gathering information in many ways, including from:

- National market and home price statistics.
- Local news that influences real estate, prices, and rents.
- Research done by driving through neighborhoods.
- Specific property images, valuation data, and condition notes.

- Property listing reports, price changes, status changes and more from real estate agents.
- Foreclosure filings, courthouse data, and ownership research for abandoned properties.

There's lots more, but you're getting the idea. The successful investor is constantly monitoring their market and deal opportunities. We don't do it all at the desk on a computer either. We're mobile, visiting our flip job sites, checking out foreclosures, and developing estimates to renovate properties.

Back in the "good old days," we would have an office something like the one in the photo. File cabinets stuffed full of folders and a lot of dead trees. We would spend a lot of time trying to figure out the best place to file that piece of paper with the data about a foreclosure. Even the most organized of us would still spend too much time trying to find that piece of paper later.

Then computers and databases came along, and things got a bit better. We could put notes and information into a folder on our hard drive. We could do the same with our email system, filing emails by subject or content into folders. It got a little bit easier to find things, as it didn't involve paper cuts. But there were still notes and emails we filed into one folder, and we tried to find them in another one later because we were thinking differently that day.

Even more of a problem for the mobile real estate investor, we didn't have that desktop computer with us in the field. Sure, notebook computers and smart phones help, but we're still dumping information into a bunch of different data buckets.

### *Challenge:*

Developing an information-gathering and filing system that makes it fast and easy to get a lot of information from many different sources into one place. Getting this information into the system from wherever we happen to be and with whatever data tool we have at the time is next. Finally, being able to find that single data item quickly when we need it is critical.

*Solution:*

The ideal solution would be a tool that captures data on our hard drive, backs it up online, and does so from our desk or on the go. This system would include capturing emails, field notes, attached documents, and even images. It would be easily searched from any of our devices, popping up the precise item of information we need. Everything on our drive is also in the cloud, so we can use a computer or smart phone anywhere to access our files.

## *EVERNOTE* is That Tool

Evernote is an online and software resource for capturing notes. It has developed over time to be a tool used by more than 10 million people. Starting with our first requirement, here are the ways in which you can get data and documents into Evernote:

- Web browser clipping of pages or selected text and images you find on the Internet.

- A special email address to forward emails into your notebooks.

- Typing notes and attaching documents directly into the system.

- With apps for iPhone and Android to type notes, take photos, and forward information from the field.

- Right-click menu on your computer to file away selected text on your screen from just about any software you have open.

- Using third party apps and equipment, you can scan notes into Evernote, even using scanning apps on smart phones.

- Voice notes that convert to text when you record the notes on your smart phone.

There are others, but these are the most popular ones. We've met the first challenge by making it fast and easy to get information into the system from anywhere we are.

Our next challenge is finding information when we need it. Evernote's search tools are every bit as good inside the system as Google is on the Web. There are two ways you group or catalog information: notebooks and tags. You can then search on tags within notebooks and zero in on what you want.

**Example:** You have a notebook for foreclosure homes you're considering for purchase. Instead of trying to set up notebooks for every subdivision or neighborhood, you can use the neighborhood name as a tag. Later you can find the foreclosures in an area by neighborhood or zip code with a simple tag search in the foreclosure notebook.

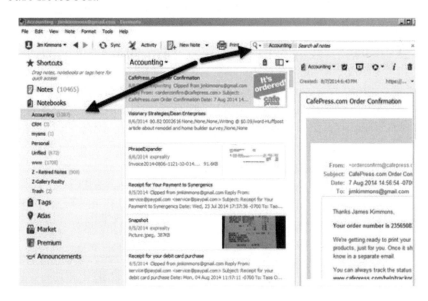

We do a lot of our communication these days with email. Using a special Evernote email address, you can forward emails into your filing system, even specifying the notebook and tagging the email as well. Using our previous example, an email from our contractor with an estimate of repairs on a foreclosure property can be forwarded into the foreclosure file and tagged with "repairs," or "estimates," or multiple tags of your choosing. Since the address would be in the document or email, you can find every estimate for work on that property with a search of the address and "estimates" tag.

You can also save searches, so if you're doing the same search over and over, just save it for one-click access later. If you're working on a flip, and you're sending all of your purchase receipts and invoices into Evernote, you can save a search for all of the costs associated with an address search and the tag "jobcost."

### *Additional Premium Features*

So far, all of these features are available in the free version of Evernote. There are limits for the storage space you upload in a month (no limit on overall space for notes), but it's pretty generous. You may want to consider paying the small $45/year cost to upgrade to premium for some extra features. You get a greater monthly upload allowance, but you also get some features that come in handy:

- **Image text recognition** – You're out cruising a neighborhood and you see a for sale sign on a property. You have an interest, so you take a quick photo of the front of the property, and another of the for sale sign. Premium Evernote will recognize the text in the sign so you can do a search later on the agent or company name and the image will display so you can call them.
- **Text indexing inside attached pdf and document files** – Sending emails with pdf file attachments will have the added value of the text inside the attached file being indexed. Any search on words or phrases in these files will display the note and attached document with your search phrase highlighted.

- **Business cards too** – Taking a photo of business cards, Evernote will index the text. Later, if you want to find the phone number for that appraiser you met at the last investment club meeting, you can search on "appraiser," or "appraisal," and whatever else you remember about them, like their first name. If you're tagging business card photos with "contact" or "card," you can search for that tag with "appraisal" to narrow things down a bit as well.
- **Handwritten notes:** You can hand write notes on your tablet computer or smart phone, and Evernote will index the words in the note. It won't recognize every word, especially if you're a doctor, but most will later make your handwritten notes searchable.

As we go through the strategies and activities of real estate investing in detail, I'll mention specific things you can do to capture information you need into Evernote. Of course, feel free to carry around a notebook and do it the good old-fashioned way if you want.

The question to ask yourself is whether your time is more valuable in digging through paper files or in working up an offer on your next deal. Check out Evernote.com.

---

### Perspectives & Progress

Whatever you decide about Evernote, now is the time to build your information filing system and a plan to capture, save, and locate information later. In the next chapter, we'll be learning about market research, valuation calculations, and specific investment strategies.

The more properties you view, vendors you work with, and offers you make, the more you need to be efficient in your systems. Your profits and success will increase if you spend less time benefitting from more information.

*Chapter 6*

---

## Be the Market Expert the Realtors Call

*"Research is formalized curiosity. It is poking and prying with a purpose." – Zora Neale Hurston*

You're setting out with a mission to build a successful real estate investment business. You're poking and prying at your market with that purpose: to create success and profits. You'll be using real estate agents a lot in your new business to help you leverage your activities and do more deals. But the average real estate agent is so busy in the trenches writing contracts, nursing their clients through the process, and going to closings, that they aren't always up-to-date on the big picture of the local market.

It's your business, you're the boss, and you want to make the big picture decisions about areas in which to invest, homes that will sell, and how much you can pay to get the profits you want. Letting real estate agents tell you that XYZ neighborhood is the "hot place to buy," or that a home is a steal at the listed price can be a mistake.

Time is money, and before the Internet successful investors spent a lot of time conducting market research. The Web has changed our business for the better, and using online resources we can stay on top of the market with a lot less digging, poking, and prying. This chapter is going to prove invaluable to you. Some of the information you'll gather will come from the local MLS, Multiple Listing Service, maintained by the real estate agents. You'll just do more with it and you'll be someone the agents call for market intelligence. Using these tools and resources, you won't spend a lot of time gathering intelligence, either.

## Big Picture with a Local Perspective

There are two major sources of home price and value data used by the government, home builders, real estate professionals, and investors. Let's get an overview of what they tell us and how they're different, even though they're publishing similar price information. The good news is that you can have a link to their monthly reports sent to you in an email which you can scan for national trends and then zero in on your market area.

### S&P Case-Shiller Home Price Index

If you really want to know how home prices are trending, you want to compare apples to apples. This home price index does that by comparing repeat sales of the same home over time. There's no better way to see how home prices in an area are moving than to watch the sales by address. By excluding homes that have had major modifications or improvements between sales, the index attempts to evaluate just the price movement between sales.

From the website: *"The S&P/Case-Shiller Home Price Indices are calculated monthly using a three-month moving average. Index levels are published with a two-month lag and are released at 9 am EST on the last Tuesday of every month. The S&P/Case-Shiller U.S. National Home Price Index is calculated quarterly and levels are published in*

*February, May, August, and November, also with a two-month lag. Index performance is based on non-seasonally adjusted data."*

The S&P/Case-Shiller 20-City Composite Home Price Index measures the value of residential real estate in 20 major U.S. metropolitan areas: Atlanta, Boston, Charlotte, Chicago, Cleveland, Dallas, Denver, Detroit, Las Vegas, Los Angeles, Miami, Minneapolis, New York, Phoenix, Portland, San Diego, San Francisco, Seattle, Tampa, and Washington, D.C.

The index gathers the sales data once it's publicly available at local recording offices around the country. You will find a national index as well as a 10-city model. Subscribing to this monthly or just visiting the site each month, you can get a big picture view of how home prices are moving. If you're in one of the measured markets, it's even better.

## FHFA, Federal Housing Finance Agency House Price Index

From the website: *The HPI is a broad measure of the movement of single-family house prices. The HPI is a weighted, repeat-sales index, meaning that it measures average price changes in repeat sales or refinancings on the same properties. This information is obtained by reviewing repeat mortgage transactions on single-family properties whose mortgages have been purchased or securitized by Fannie Mae or Freddie Mac since January 1975.*

*The HPI serves as a timely, accurate indicator of house price trends at various geographic levels. Because of the breadth of the sample, it provides more information than is available in other house price indexes. It also provides housing economists with an improved analytical tool that is useful for estimating changes in the rates of mortgage defaults, prepayments and housing affordability in specific geographic areas.*

*The HPI includes house price figures for the nine Census Bureau divisions, for the 50 states and the District of Columbia, and for Metropolitan Statistical Areas (MSAs) and Divisions.*

Notice the difference between this index and Case-Shiller. While FHFA is also tracking repeat sales of the same homes, the data comes from mortgage information from transactions involving federally insured home loans. Since the vast majority of home loans are guaranteed in some way by one of the federal agencies, this is an accurate set of data. And, as the site says, there is a lot more available and for many more areas.

Since refinancing and new purchases involve different motivations and market considerations, such as interest rates, this index publishes two versions: 1) All transactions, and 2) New purchases only.

**Table 1: Monthly Price Change Estimates for U.S. and Census Divisions**
(Purchase-Only Index, Seasonally Adjusted)

| | U.S. | Pacific | Mountain | West North Central | West South Central | East North Central | East South Central | New England | Middle Atlantic | South Atlantic |
|---|---|---|---|---|---|---|---|---|---|---|
| **Apr 14 - May 14** | **0.4%** | **0.2%** | **0.4%** | **0.6%** | **1.1%** | **-0.1%** | **-0.7%** | **0.8%** | **1.1%** | **0.2%** |
| Mar 14 - Apr 14 | 0.1% | 0.0% | 0.0% | 0.0% | -0.6% | 0.4% | 0.6% | -1.1% | 0.6% | 0.4% |
| (Previous Estimate) | 0.0% | -0.1% | -0.4% | 0.1% | -0.6% | 0.5% | 0.6% | -1.3% | 0.2% | 0.3% |
| Feb 14 - Mar 14 | 0.6% | 0.5% | -0.1% | 1.1% | 0.6% | 1.1% | -0.3% | 3.7% | 0.3% | 0.4% |
| (Previous Estimate) | 0.7% | 0.6% | -0.1% | 1.2% | 0.5% | 1.2% | -0.2% | 4.1% | 0.9% | 0.3% |
| Jan 14 - Feb 14 | 0.6% | 1.5% | 1.1% | 0.2% | 1.0% | 0.5% | 0.5% | -1.4% | -0.7% | 1.1% |
| (Previous Estimate) | 0.5% | 1.3% | 1.1% | 0.2% | 1.0% | 0.4% | 0.4% | -2.0% | -0.9% | 1.0% |
| Dec 13 - Jan 14 | 0.3% | 0.6% | 0.6% | 0.9% | -0.5% | -0.2% | 0.5% | 0.8% | 1.5% | -0.1% |
| (Previous Estimate) | 0.4% | 0.8% | 0.6% | 0.9% | -0.4% | -0.1% | 0.5% | 1.3% | 1.5% | -0.1% |
| Nov 13 - Dec 13 | 0.8% | 0.7% | 0.6% | 0.4% | 2.0% | 0.9% | 1.4% | -1.0% | -1.2% | 1.4% |
| (Previous Estimate) | 0.7% | 0.7% | 0.6% | 0.3% | 1.6% | 0.9% | 1.4% | -1.1% | -1.1% | 1.4% |
| **12-Month Change:** | | | | | | | | | | |
| May 13 - May 14 | 5.5% | 9.6% | 8.4% | 5.3% | 5.3% | 4.6% | 3.2% | 2.6% | 2.5% | 5.4% |

The image shows the nine Census Divisions monthly chart, which shows the movement of prices as well as a 12-month change. It's a very fast way to get an overview of larger areas. But the major advantage of this index is that it also tracks hundreds of smaller cities and towns. Your local area, or one close to you, is probably tracked.

### Lagging Data

Both of these indexes must gather and compile past sales data, so they are running at least 45 days behind for monthly reports. But it's a great way to get a quick look at what prices are doing in the near past. It's also a good tool if you're considering investing in different areas, as you can compare their price movements for decisions. Subscribe for email alerts and take the links to the full reports to get a big picture overview in just minutes each month.

{**Evernote**} This is a really good use of Evernote, as you can create a notebook for your area and perhaps name it "Market Stats."

Save these reports directly to that notebook from the screen, and you'll be building a great file of market history you may need to refer to for investment decisions.

## Local Government & Organizations

There is nothing more influential in real estate price movement than local planning, zoning, and development activities. Whole neighborhoods can see big swings in values up or down based on decisions to develop a green area/park or an industrial park nearby. You'll want to attend zoning meetings or get copies of notes of the meetings to make area investment decisions.

The local chamber of commerce is another great resource. If you join, they'll send you announcements of expansions planned by their members. Learning early about a new shopping mall expansion or location could give you an edge in buying before prices rise. If their dues are more than you want to pay, you can just keep track on their websites, as they tend to promote their members well.

A local home builders' association can be a wonderful early alert system for new development or promising neighborhoods. Builders, particularly spec home builders, are one of your best resources. By tracking established areas where they're building or nearby development, you can target neighborhoods for investment.

In the next chapter we'll talk about another local resource: real estate investment clubs. You can meet people who are movers and shakers in the local real estate market, but these are even better marketing tools as you'll see.

## MLS, Multiple Listing Service, Automated Reporting

Almost every area now has a computerized MLS used by real estate brokers to market their listings and share commissions with brokers who bring buyers. Computers and the Web make it easy for a real estate agent to create automated reports of home sales for email delivery. If you can find a local agent website with a full-featured MLS search tool, you can even create your own reports.

### *IDX, Internet Data Exchange*

The IDX is an agreement between the broker members of an MLS to allow their listings to be displayed on all member broker websites. This way you can search through listed homes on any IDX member's site and you're seeing all of the members' listings. No longer do you need to go to every brokerage site to view just their listings.

Search on Google with "yourtown mls idx" to pull up websites with IDX search functions. Using "idx" in the search, you'll get the right sites because there is a required IDX disclosure on the search pages. Just keep going to these sites until you find one that allows registration to create your own searches and email alerts. This gives you the ability to:

- Build custom searches for different sets of criteria and neighborhoods.
- Create searches just for new listings and price changes.
- Create sold property searches, if allowed in your MLS, to keep track of sold prices by area.
- Get these alerts delivered by email.

## Search Taos County Listings

**Check next to the padlock image below to register to save your searches and get email alerts!**

The image shows a partial screenshot from a real estate website with the features you want to find in your area. You see that you can even save listings if you're watching a particular home for changes. You can create searches for neighborhoods or zip codes and get constant automated reporting of what's going on in the market. You'll probably be contacted by the site owner because you become an identified prospect when you register. Just tell them what you're doing and you may create a new relationship for future business.

In some areas the IDX will not show you sold properties, and it may even be a privacy issue in others. However, if you contact the agent, they can usually create a report for you that will deliver sold reports as they are posted by members. You'll see some valuable information, such as the amount the home sold for, but also how much sold prices are running below list prices. In most cases you'll also be able to see how long a home is on the market (DOM – Days on Market) before it sells. This information may also be broken down into DOM for different price ranges.

{**Evernote**} Nearly everything we've discussed here is delivered via a link to a website or a PDF document. It's just a click or two to have it filed away for easy retrieval. The Premium version of Evernote will index the text in PDF documents, which is great if the MLS reports are delivered that way.

You can search by address and pull up every note, site page, or document related to a specific property. Links saved from a site to Evernote will be live and clickable.

Once you've accumulated months of sold property reports, it's great to be able to search on the keywords in the reports that indicate a sold property and the area. An example might be "Sold price" or "AreaName" as a search. You can even specify number of bedrooms or other features to narrow the results. You'll have all of the sold properties pop up in reverse order with the most recent at the top. When we get to the chapter about doing CMAs, Comparative Market Analysis, to value properties, this gets you some fast access to recent comps.

## Don't Make this a Major Task

The best thing about computers, MLS capability, and online document storage is that it helps us to gather, categorize, and file information so that it is available when we need it. You should use the tools that work best for you so that you don't have to spend a lot of time capturing and storing information. Then when it's time to use it, you should have a fast and easy way to grab what you need, even if you're not at your desk.

---

### Perspectives & Progress

Use as many or as few of these tips as you believe are necessary to your chosen strategies and business success. You may be able to get by without national or statewide real estate price data, and if that's the case, it's great if you're making money.

I do know that when I am trying to make an investment decision and doubts creep into my head, having some hard data to guide me can help. The more you know, the better you'll sleep at night when you're buying and selling properties.

---

### Chapter 7

## *For Every Seller There's a Buyer.*
## *You Need Both*

*"The buyer needs a hundred eyes, the seller but one." – George Herbert*

Before we jump into the mechanics of real estate investing, you'll need to get the marketing down. You're about to delve into valuation of properties and your role in the various real estate investment strategies. You can be:

- A buyer of properties.
- A seller of properties.
- Both the buyer and the seller of a property.
- A middle person or wholesaler with no ownership role.

As you can see, you have various ways to make money investing in real estate, which is why it's a great business. But look back at those roles and you'll see a common thread. You will need sellers if you're a buyer, and buyers if you're a seller, and both if you're a wholesaler or middle person in a transaction.

## Understanding your Role & Value

We're going into great detail in future chapters about the specific things you do to establish your value to buyers and sellers of real estate. Sellers are individual homeowners, usually in some distress and needing help to sell their homes. They can also be banks holding foreclosures. Buyers can be retail buyers or more often long-term real estate investors, and you're flipping or wholesaling to them.

George Herbert's quote at the beginning of this chapter is really very appropriate for what we're learning and applying here. The buyer needs a hundred eyes because they have a great many "due diligence" tasks to make sure that they are getting precisely what they expect in a purchase and not paying more than they should for it. On the other side, the seller really only needs one, as their sole focus is on getting out from under a property, whether they're the homeowner or a bank holding a foreclosure.

Understanding this, you can effectively market to build your "buyer list," and to locate motivated sellers. Let's look at the various marketing methods and venues to see how each is used for both buyer and seller marketing. Once you understand the value you bring to the table, you can market that value and begin to build a strong list of eager buyers waiting for you to deliver properties. You'll also be working with sellers who need your help and buying at discounts to current market value.

## Newspapers

This old tried-and-true medium is still around because it works. The use of newspapers by real estate investors has changed somewhat over time, simply due to other online tools that provide the same service at less expense. However, you may still want to use classified ads, as there are people who really like to read the paper who aren't computer users.

To use classified ads effectively, you need to understand that they should be regular, uninterrupted, and in the same general location at all times. You have no idea when a buyer or seller may suddenly have a need for your services. By keeping ads in place regularly, you'll be sure that the ad is there when they need it. They may even come looking for it, as they've seen it every time they've read that section of the classifieds. You have become "top-of-mind" precisely when you want to be.

### Buyers

You can reach retail buyers for properties you're flipping and renovating, but classified ads really work well in reaching investor buyers. These are usually rental property investors scanning the classifieds for motivated sellers and good deals.

You'll be a really happy and profitable real estate investor when you've managed to build out a list of these buyers who buy multiple properties for investment. They're a customer base you can count on and you'll learn in this book how to deliver the right properties at the right prices so they'll be eagerly waiting for your deals.

When it comes to trying to hook up with one of these buyers, you get your first lesson in "creative marketing." It's when you run an ad something like this one without owning the home you're advertising:

> *Ready to Rent Home for Sale*
> *3 br, 2 ba home in high rent*
> *area, but priced to move.*
> *[contact info]*

There are a dozen variations for the wording of this ad, but the important thing is that it attracts the interest of the targeted investor. What's this about not owning the home? You don't have to own this home, or even know where one might be. Your goal is to get the investor to contact you. At that point, you apologize that the ad was about to be stopped since the home has sold. You tell them that you specialize in locating motivated sellers with good rental homes, so please let you contact them, as you're working a few deals now.

Will they be suspicious of this approach? Maybe. But even some of those who are may give you their contact info anyway because you seem to be an enterprising investor and a possible resource for good deals. They may ask a few questions to see if you know what you're talking about, and you will be knowledgeable once you've read this book. If a conversation starts, you should also ask them some questions to help you understand the type of properties they want and in what areas so that you can place them on your buyer list.

{**Evernote**} This is a very good use for Evernote. Make notes of your conversation and their contact info and place them into your "Buyer" notebook. Every time you interact with them in the future, do the same. You'll be building a detailed file of their preferences and how they do deals. When it comes to the areas and types of property they want, you need this information in the file. Later you can search in the Buyer notebook by area and/or property type to find the right buyers for a home you're negotiating to buy.

### Sellers

While those buyers will need a hundred eyes, when you market for sellers, they only want that one thing: a home sold, and quickly. They could be unable to continue making mortgage payments, maybe already have received a default notice, or may even be in the pre-foreclosure stage. It doesn't matter as long as they still have control and the ability to sell. They are definitely motivated to do so. You won't know if a property will work for you until you get more details, but you can't get them until a seller contacts you.

> *I Buy Houses for Cash*
> *Need to sell but having trouble?*
> *One phone call and you may*
> *have just the home I need.*
> *[contact info]*

You can run different variations of this ad, maybe one with a specific area targeted and headlined *"I need to buy homes for cash in XXXXXX Subdivision."* You don't need to have the money to buy either. In the chapter on Assignments, you'll learn how to lock up control of a home with little cash and no obligation to buy.

### You Need Buyers First

Unless you're buying for your own rental investing needs, you must have qualified buyers on your list before you advertise for sellers. You don't want to waste time and money advertising only to have to pass on an amazing deal because you can't find a buyer in time to lock up the deal with the seller. This rule applies to all of your marketing activities.

## Craigslist

Craigslist is sometimes known as "classifieds on steroids." First, it's free to use, so that gives it a leg up right away. But there's another slam dunk reason for using Craigslist: it's online and searchable.

Everything discussed in the newspaper classified material applies to Craigslist with only slight modification. Because Craigslist is searchable, you'll want to use phrases in your ads that people are using to search for properties to buy or buyers for their homes. You'll also see that other investors are doing the same thing. Here are some ad title examples in the "Real Estate Wanted" category:

- Facing foreclosure? Don't walk away. There are options.
- I buy [neighborhood] homes for cash in 30 days.
- Lease with Option to Buy. Low Down

You advertise for sellers and buyers similar to what we discussed in the newspaper classifieds, but now using phrases like:

- Need to sell
- Must sell fast
- Avoid foreclosure
- Buying homes cash
- Lease to own
- Lease purchase
- Rent to own
- Rental home for sale
- Home for sale as rental
- Fast cash for homes

With some thought and by checking out Craigslist in your area, you can come up with more. The point is that your prospects don't have to read over pages of classifieds. They type in their search, and you pop up. You can do the same, searching for "must sell" type ads.

Here's a partial screenshot of search results in "Real Estate For Sale," with results limited to "by owner."

★ Rio Rancho Land - 1 ACRE - $2499 (Rio Rancho) pic map

★ Ohio Investment Property - $24900 / 3br - 1500ft² - (Campbell) pic map

★ NE Heights 3 BR NEW EVERYTHING!! - $229000 / 3br - 1587ft² - (Montgomery/Wyoming) pic

★ HOME FOR SALE by OWNER - $139 / 3br - 1350ft² - (2708 Alamogordo NW) pic map

★ Rio Rancho Land near electric - 1/2 ACRE - $2499 (Rio Rancho) pic map

★ TEXAS HORSE RANCH FOR SALE - $750000 / 5br - 4300ft² - (BROCK) pic map

★ Land for sale! - $15000 map

★ 10 acres south of Moriarty - map

★ Lovely Candlelight home - $280500 / 3br - 1620ft² - (1893 Candela Street) pic map

★ Seven Acre Ranch in Glorieta -- Owner Finance Available - (Outside Santa Fe) pic map

★ Lease to own mobile home $630. a month - $630 / 2br - 859ft² - (3000 Aztec Park) map

★ Nice lot to build on - (north valley)

Limiting to "by owner" should kick out most of the Realtor listings and other investor ads. Craigslist is free, so use it.

## Real Estate Investment Clubs

Joining a local real estate investment club is a form of marketing. You're going to more than just investors. Members of these clubs include:

- Realtors
- Appraisers
- Inspectors
- Surveyors
- Mortgage Brokers

- Contractors
- Property Managers

You can learn a lot in these clubs, compare notes and strategies with other investors, and actually connect with buyers you can add to your list. Active rental property buyers join these clubs to meet wholesalers and fix & flip investors.

Do a Google search on "real estate investment clubs" for some national associations with listings in your area. You can also short-circuit that with a search on "yourtown real estate investment club."

## Bandit Signs

You've seen these small signs in subdivisions and on street corners. They're not as long as classified ads, but they have similar headlines such as "I buy houses fast for cash [contact info]."

Check your local laws and subdivision rules before planting these signs, or they'll disappear and you may be fined. If there is a town or county law against them, you can sometimes get away with posting them over the weekend and picking them up Sunday evening. Government employees aren't working then.

| I Buy Homes For Cash [contact] | Sell Your Home Fast For Cash [contact] | Sell Fast - Avoid- Foreclosure [contact] | Cash for Your Home 30 Days [contact] | Don't Foreclosure Sell for Cash [contact] |
|---|---|---|---|---|

These little signs work, so check the rules and areas of opportunity in your market. Think outside the box and avoid being one of many on a corner if you can. Watch traffic patterns and choose a less busy corner but one with traffic. Fewer drivers may pass, but you may have more success if your sign is standing alone.

## Local Bulletin Boards

This is a marketing strategy good for finding motivated sellers. When you see a supermarket, school, or other place with bulletin boards posting homes for sale or rent, you may find some seller candidates. They may be in trouble and needing to sell without real estate commissions, or they've been unable to sell and are trying to rent out the home.

You can call on those cards, and you can (check the board rules if any) post your "I buy houses for cash" card on the board. Use the little "tear-off" phone numbers so they can take them along. You can also check interest when you come back by seeing how many numbers are gone.

## Website

The Internet has become almost a necessity for anyone wanting serious consideration as a business. The good news is that you can have a nice website absolutely free of charge if you want to do a bit of work to build it. *WordPress.com* is where to go to set up a free site, with no cost for Web hosting. You'll get a domain address like http://yourname.wordpress.com. However, if you want your own domain name like http://yournameinvesting.com, you can pay around $12/year to *GoDaddy* or *Yahoo* and point it at your Word-Press.com site.

There are dozens of great "dummy" type books to learn Word-Press. If you make a serious effort, you can have a website up and running with good content in under a couple of weeks. You can then put your domain name in ads and on signs. People tend to be more likely to call you if they can check you out on a website first.

What is good content for the site? It's what you do and how it helps sellers to sell homes and investors to buy right for excellent ROI, Return on Investment. You just write about how you do what you do and post about deals you've done and how they helped someone to sell when they hadn't been successful before, etc.

You can do market reports, as everybody likes statistics. You can post photo slideshows of homes you've bought and sold as well as fix & flip projects. This shows you are active and know what you're doing. Don't worry so much about whether you get good search engine exposure, because that's very hard to do. Your website is a secondary marketing tool that shows your expertise and experience to build trust.

## Social Websites

These are sites like *Facebook, Twitter, Google+, LinkedIn, YouTube, Instagram,* and *Pinterest.* Feel free to build profiles on these sites and do some posting there and link back to your website for exposure. I wouldn't count on much direct business, as people don't participate on these sites to do real estate business.

LinkedIn is an exception. It's a business-oriented site, and you could actually get a deal from participation in some of the real estate investment groups.

**Real Estate** Investment Guild: **Investors**, Capital Raising, Fund Formation & Fund Administration
The Real Estate Investment Guild is a 40,000 member association of investment professionals and investors. Connect ...
Very Active: 346 discussions this month · 40,628 members
▸ 6,540 in your network · Similar

CREPIG - Commercial **Real Estate** Professionals & **Investors** Group
CRE Investors, Property Owners & Professionals. Find and Finance projects, Industry information. Jobs, Attorney, CPA's ...
Very Active: 687 discussions this month · 19,828 members
▸ 4,216 in your network · Similar

**Real Estate Investors** Referral Network
This is a group where real estate Investors can get together and discuss their experiences, future plans, and areas of ...
Very Active: 563 discussions this month · 10,326 members
▸ 3,183 in your network · Similar

International **Real Estate Investors** Group
This is an International Real Estate Investors Group integrated for all real estate professional around the world: INVESTORS...
18 discussions this month · 5,000 members
▸ 1,076 in your network · Similar

The **Real Estate Investors**, Developers & Professionals Forum - Powered by ClarkeFunds.com
🔒 This group is for the purpose of connecting real estate investors and professionals all over the globe. Networking, deal ...

A search on "real estate investors" turned up many results, a few of which are shown in the screenshot above. Notice that there is a referral network, so some future business may be a possibility. At the very least, you can be a member of an extended group of non-competitors. This makes discussion of specific strategies possible.

YouTube can be a great marketing tool to link back to your website, especially if you do fix & flip. Make video clips of progress as you turn an ugly duckling house into a beautiful home. People love video, and they'll definitely see that you know your stuff.

Behind the scenes of "Flipping Vegas!"
by MommyReporter • 2 months ago • 4,073 views
Check out more pics and info here: http://www.mommyreporter.com/behind-the-scenes-flipping-vegas-scott-yancey-review-live/ ...
HD

## Good Old-fashioned Networking

Grab a pile of business cards and visit banks, mortgage brokers, credit unions, real estate brokerages, investment brokers and groups, home shows, and anywhere else you could meet a prospective buyer or seller.

Offer to give instructional talks to groups who have members interested in retirement investment. You'll be giving them information about owning rental properties, and you'll be adding buyers to your list at the same time.

## Go Forward with Marketing in Mind

Now you're ready to get into the nuts and bolts of real estate investing. As you go through the rest of the book, be make notes about how what you're learning can be used in your marketing to show that you are the local real estate expert.

## Perspectives & Progress

Start noticing marketing opportunities around you. Make note of neighborhood bulletin boards, subdivision newsletters, home owner association websites, etc. You can offer to write a short article for other real estate local publications or websites or ask to trade links with homeowner association or subdivision websites.

Start a marketing plan. Check out newspaper advertising rates, and start a website if you think you want to and are able to do that. Set up a LinkedIn profile as a real estate investor.

---

### Chapter 8

# *It's Only a Good Deal if the Numbers Work*

*"Price ain't merely about numbers. It's a satisfying sacrifice."*
*– Toba Beta*

Before we dig into investment calculations, read the quote above again, because it's important. It's very true that a real estate investment can be less profitable than expected if we don't "run the numbers" properly before going into the deal. But making decisions just on the numbers isn't the best approach, either.

The numbers on a rental home purchase can look great for cash flow and ROI when the price is deeply discounted. However, if the home is in a declining area with people moving away, then the numbers won't last and we'll be locked into a failing investment. So price is a "satisfying sacrifice" of money for peace of mind in an investment. We need both the numbers and some expectation that they'll continue or even improve in the future.

That said, the calculations in this chapter may apply to one or more of the strategies you're using, or they may not. This is an overview and explanation of the most commonly used real estate investment calculations and their purpose in valuation. You should have some understanding of them, but don't hyperventilate over them if you're not good at math. At the end of the chapter, there are some links to spreadsheets I found that can do much of the heavy lifting for you. Some of these can also be done for you with a financial calculator.

## Simple and Compound Interest

There are plenty of online calculators and smartphone apps that will do these interest calculations for you, but if you want to have a basic understanding of why the results come out the way they do, here are some quick explanations and examples:

### Simple Interest

Simple interest is paid over time based only on the amount originally invested. An example would be a government or corporate bond that you purchase for $5,000 with a rate of return of 6% simple interest. Each year until maturity, you would receive 6% of $5,000, or $300/year. If you want to see the return for more than three years, here's the calculation:

$$\$5,000 \times [1 + (.06 \times 3)]$$
$$\$5,000 \times [1 + .18]$$
$$\$5,000 \times 1.18 = \$5,900$$

Of course you math wizards may have just multiplied 3 x $300/year, but that's the math behind simple interest.

### Compound Interest

Compounding of interest is paying interest on interest, which is a good deal for the investor. Using our example above, if interest is compounded annually, we would be changing the amount on which the interest is calculated each year. Let's do that for this example for three years:

*Year 1: $5,000 X .06 = $300*

*Year 2: $5,300 X .06 = $318*

*Year 3: $5618 X .06 = $337*

*At the end of three years, our investment is now $5,955.*

Earning interest on interest is great, especially if the compounding is done more frequently. Many investments compound monthly, and some even more frequently.

## Buy and Sell Side Real Estate Calculations

These calculations are involved in evaluating a property for purchase and profit from sale, as well as three popular calculations used by lenders to decide whether to loan money and how much.

### *Real Estate Purchase Costs*

| Settlement Service | Charge or Range of Charges |
|---|---|
| Abstract or Title Search | $40 - $175 |
| Settlement or Closing | $150 - $700 |
| Flood Hazard Area Determination | $6 - $11 |
| Title Insurance and Title Exam | See page 2 |
| Tax Information Report | $35 |
| Construction Site Inspection | $75 - $700 |
| Settlement Coordination | $38 |
| CEM Closing Coordination | $250 |
| Tax Service | $75 - $90 |
| Mortgage Loan | See page 4 |
| Homeowners Insurance | See page 3 |

This is really less of a calculation than a checklist to make sure you don't miss some of the closing and other costs involved in a real estate purchase. You should always ask for a lender's disclosure early to see what loan costs will be, as they are normally the largest dollar category in the closing HUD Statement.

- **Purchase Price + Concessions**
  - The negotiated price to buy the property.
  - Any concessions you've made to the Seller, such as paying some of their closing costs.

- **Financing Costs**
  - If you're flipping with transaction financing, you'll have the costs of the short-term loan.
  - All long-term mortgage loan costs, such as points, origination fees, credit report, etc. Usually the appraisal fee is in this group.
  - Any special appraisal or re-appraisal fees paid outside the loan costs.

- **Closing Costs**
  - Negotiated title insurance costs, since it varies as to whether the buyer or seller pays. These include the title insurance binder fee, the abstract fee, and the title insurance policy premium.
  - Negotiated survey cost, as it's customary in some areas for the seller to pay for survey.
  - Buyer side attorney fees, if any.
  - Buyer side recording fees, such as recording the mortgage at the courthouse.
  - Any local government or homeowner association transfer fees.
  - Homeowner association (or condo association) dues/fees pro-rated for the portion of the first year you'll own the property.
  - Pro-rated property taxes for the portion of the year you'll own the property. This can be a credit, if taxes have not yet been paid for the year. The seller will credit you with the portion they owe so you can pay it at the time taxes are billed.
  - Payment of homeowner insurance premium through

the end of the year or other specified time frame.

- ○ Fee charged by the title company to handle the transaction. Sometimes it is customary for the buyer and seller to split this.
- ○ Attorney fee to prepare the deed, negotiable but the seller usually pays.
- ○ You'll owe the interest until the first payment. If you buy with a mortgage and close on the 15th of June, normally your first payment will be the 1st of August. You'll be paying the remaining 15 or so days of interest for June, and your first payment will pay July's interest.
- ○ Any city, county, or state fees or tax stamps as negotiated between you and the seller.
- ○ Any postage, courier, or FedEx/UPS fees for document deliveries.

Depending on where you are, there can be lower or higher closing costs. Early on you should get a preliminary Truth in Lending disclosure and HUD statement with estimated costs.

Remember that this isn't what you'll have to bring to closing, as the cash you must provide then will be reduced by whatever earnest money you deposited up front but increased by any escrows required by the lender. They often want money escrowed for taxes and insurance for several months to a year in advance. These are costs, but they're costs incurred later, as for now they're sitting in an escrow account. It's still out-of-pocket expense, though.

### *Costs in the Sale of the Property*

You can use the line items above as a guide, as the negotiable items would apply to the seller side of the HUD statement. Frequently the seller is paying for the survey, and probably the title insurance policy premium. It varies significantly around the country, usually due to local taxing and real estate stamps, but a reasonable sliding rule-of-thumb is that the seller's closing costs will be between 5% and 8% of the sale price if a mortgage is involved.

If the sale is profitable, the cash received at closing will be reduced by the amount needed to pay off the mortgage and closing costs. This of course will be the proceeds before taxes, as Uncle Sam and maybe the state will still want their cut. Rolling the sale into another property with a 1031 tax deferred exchange would reduce or eliminate this outlay.

## Lender Calculations for Mortgages

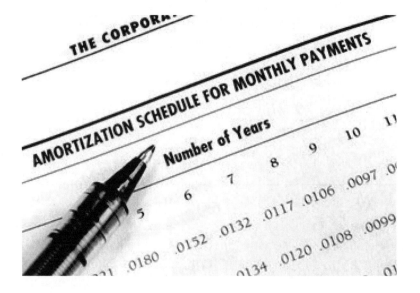

When you need a mortgage to purchase an investment property, the lender will use various methods to determine if they'll loan you money, and how much they're willing to loan on the property. Of course, they'll do credit checks (not for some commercial and apartment deals), an appraisal, and they'll examine your assets and liabilities as well. Generally, the Loan-To-Value ratio is used for single family and small multiple unit loan evaluations, while the Debt Coverage and Break-Even Ratios are used for commercial and multi-family mortgages.

### *Loan-To-Value (LTV) Ratio*

This is the ratio of the amount to be borrowed against the value of the property. There will be a limit, often 80%, over which most lenders will not do the loan. This would be a maximum loan of $80,000 on a purchase price of $100,000, which means you'll be making a 20% down payment. This is protection for the lender in case of default, as they hope to have enough equity in the property to sell and get their loan balance back.

There's a hidden hitch in this that surprises some investors the first time they bump into it. You've just congratulated yourself on negotiating an awesome deal, as the market appraised value of the home is $125,000, and you got it for $99,000. The Lender uses the "lesser of value or purchase price." They'll loan you 80% (or whatever the LTV is) of the $99,000, not the appraised value.

*Using an LTV of 85%*

*Amount to loan = $99,000 X .85*

*Loan Amount = $84,150*

You still made a great deal, as you really have more than a 20% equity if the appraisal came in at $125,000, but your lender has more downside protection.

### Debt Coverage Ratio

This is a calculation important to borrowers on commercial and multi-family properties. The lender uses this ratio to determine if your net operating income (NOI) from the property will cover the mortgage payments. The idea is to make sure that you'll be able to make those mortgage payments with a cushion.

*Debt Coverage Ratio = Annual NOI / Annual Debt Service*

If your yearly NOI on a 20 unit apartment project is $60,000, and your annual debt service (total of all payments for the year) is $48,000 ($4,000/month x 12 months), here's the calculation.

$$Debt\ Coverage\ Ratio = \$60,000 / \$48,000$$

$$Debt\ Coverage\ Ratio = 1.25$$

This project is bringing in 25% more in NOI cash than required to pay the mortgage payments. A common lender requirement is a Debt Coverage Ratio of at least 1.20, so this example deal looks like a go.

Don't worry about how NOI is calculated, as it is explained later in this chapter.

### Break-Even Ratio

This is another ratio used by lenders mostly for commercial deals. It is used to see how risky the loan might be if problems develop, such as declining rents or higher than expected vacancy rates over a long period.

$$Break\text{-}Even\ Ratio\ (BER) = (Debt\ Service + Operating\ Expenses) / Gross\ Operating\ Income$$

We'll be going through operating expenses and Gross Operating Income in this chapter. But for now, the lender wants to see how susceptible to problems the loan would be. The lender is looking for a maximum number here, meaning a lower BER number is better. Let's clarify it with an example. The operating income of an apartment project is $84,000/year. The mortgage payment is $3,200/month ($38,400/year), and the annual operating expense is $24,000. Here's the calculation:

$$BER = (\$38,400 + \$24,000) / \$84,000$$

$$BER = \$62,400 / \$84,000$$

$$BER = .74\ or\ 74\%$$

This means that the property breaks even for profit if problems cause the income to drop or expenses to rise by 26%. This is actually a pretty good number, and a common requirement of lenders is a BER of 85% or lower.

## Rental Property Income/Expense/Valuation Calculations

Rental properties run from the single family home through large apartment projects, so some of these calculations will not necessarily be used by the single family rental home investor. However, you may want to try them, and you may grow your business to the point where they all make sense.

When you're evaluating properties for rental investing, you'll use these calculations to get a comfort level with the future performance of your investment. They're roughly in the order in which you'll need them, as you'll use early calculated numbers in other calculations.

### *Gross Scheduled Income (GSI)*

This is also referred to as GPI, Gross Potential Income. It's the income before expenses or other adjustments that you expect to receive from rents at full occupancy and with the tenant(s) paying on time every month. That's in a perfect world, so this is really more of a hopeful estimate than a hard number.

Let's do an example for a single family rental home with a monthly rent of $850.

$$Gross\ Scheduled\ Income = Monthly\ Rent\ X\ 12\ Months$$

$$GPI = \$850\ X\ 12$$

$$GSI = \$10,200$$

So, in a perfect world, this rental home would bring in gross rental income of $10,200 over the year.

### Vacancy and Credit Loss (V&C Loss)

Now we're leaving the fairy tale and going back to the real world. Tenants don't always stay for years, and some leave without paying some of the rent owed. The rental property investor should factor in losses for vacant time, bad checks, and non-payment of rent, referred to as Vacancy and Credit Loss.

If you've been renting out properties in the area for a while, you'll likely have a number for this line item. It's expressed as a percentage of the gross rent expected. So, if your experience shows that the total of rents not collected due to vacancy and non-payment of rents comes to 5%, then that's the number.

In our rental home example, your Vacancy and Credit Loss estimate is $510 using the 5% estimated number. Of course you hope to do better and improve how long tenants stay and how well you collect rents. This is an estimate to help you in setting rents and calculating the worst case ROI on the property.

If you're new to this, you won't have an actual experience number, but you can possibly get a local property manager to tell you their experience. You want to try and gather enough information to keep this number realistic. Over-estimating to make you feel you're covered is not good, as it influences other decisions, such as setting the rent.

When you're considering raising rents, perhaps because the market is telling you it's safe to do so, you will want to consider if doing so will cause some stable tenants to move. If your vacancy rate increases, this can offset some or all of the rent increase, at least for the current year.

### Gross Operating Income (GOI)

Also called Effective Gross Income, this one is easy, as it just uses the first two calculations. It is the expected operating income after vacancy and credit losses and before other expenses. Using our rental home numbers, here's the calculation:

$$GOI = GSI - V\&C\ Loss$$

$$GOI = \$10,200 - \$510$$

$$GOI = \$9,690$$

If you experience lower (better) vacancy and credit losses, then your GOI increases, and the opposite if V&C Loss goes up.

### Net Operating Income (NOI)

This one gets to the heart of what you expect to keep (before Uncle Sam's bite) from your rents after all expenses are considered. As we're moving through these calculations, they're building on the others. So, we're starting this one with our Gross Operating Income (GOI). If we're estimating, then we're using our expected GOI. If the year is over, we're using our actual number after actual vacancy and credit losses.

Net Operating Income then is the GOI number minus all expenses that are annual. In other words, we would not include any property (capital) improvement costs like renovations. Those must be depreciated. We're looking for a cash available number after real annual cash paid expenses, including any or all of:

- Advertising
- Accounting
- Taxes and licenses

- Property management if we hire it out or pay ourselves
- Legal expenses
- Maintenance and repairs
- Supplies
- Office expenses
- Landscaping or yard work we pay for
- Trash removal if we pay for it
- Water and sewer fees if we pay for them
- Utilities if the tenant doesn't pay

Our rental home example has a GOI of $9690. The tenant pays all utilities and takes care of yard work. We do our own management so there are no fees for this. If we consider an attorney preparing/reviewing releases at $200/year, and minor office expenses, the total of all of our annual expenses for this property come to $2,200 with a small repair or two. Here's how our NOI is calculated:

$$NOI = GOI - Expenses$$

$$NOI = \$9,690 - \$2,200$$

$$NOI = \$7,490$$

You'll see NOI used in other calculations, as it's an important number. It's also a number over which you have some control. If you can shop better and cut some expenses, your NOI goes up, just as it does if you're able to increase rents.

### Gross Rent Multiplier (GRM)

If you're considering a number of properties for rental purchases, this is a down-and-dirty fast calculation to bring the best potential homes to the top of the list. It isn't highly accurate or detailed, so it's just for giving priority to those you want to spend more time evaluating.

Basically, it's the value/cost of the property divided by the expected or actual GOI, Gross Operating Income. If the property is already in rental service, you have a GOI number that's real. If not, it's the estimated GOI as discussed earlier. This calculation is very easy and fast, but again it's just to help you narrow down the field.

$$GRM = Cost / GOI$$

We're taking twelve months of expected or actual Gross Operating Income and dividing it into what we think we'll have to pay for the property. So if we're considering a home for purchase that's already a rental, we think we can buy it for $115,000, and the GOI is our previous example of $10,200. Here's the calculation:

$$GRM = \$115,000 / \$10,200$$

$$GRM = 11.3$$

You may be seeing that what we want here is a lower number. If we can buy another rental home for the same $115,000, but the GOI is $11,800, the GRM would be 9.75. We're getting more in gross rents for the same purchase price.

The reason this is only for narrowing down possibilities is that we don't have enough information to use it for a decision. Expenses can be very different, which can change the NOI a lot. It's the bottom line that counts. But, this will help you go through a pile of possibilities and bring the best candidates to the top for more analysis.

## Capitalization or CAP Rate

Capitalization rate is normally used for multi-family commercial properties. It's a more accurate and widely-used way to compare properties you're considering purchasing or to price a property you own for listing to sell. It's accurate and useful because it's comparing the value or cost of the property to the NOI it is generating. You're getting down to the true ROI of the property before taxes or tax breaks are considered. This allows a more accurate comparison because rents, vacancy and credit loss, and expenses are factored into the calculation.

First we'll do a basic Cap Rate calculation of a property that we may be doing when we're considering purchasing it. It's a six-plex unit with a value or purchased price of $540,000. It's generating NOI of $62,500/year.

$$Cap\ Rate = Net\ Operating\ Income\ /\ Value\ or\ Cost$$

$$Cap\ Rate = \$62,500\ /\ \$540,000$$

$$Cap\ Rate = .116,\ or\ 11.6\%$$

It's telling us that 11.6% of the value/cost of this property is generated from a year's operations. So as a buyer, we're looking for higher cap rate numbers when comparing properties, because raising the NOI or lowering the price/value would run the number up.

Let's say that we're considering several multi-family properties for purchase, and they have these cap rates:

- Property A – Cap Rate of 10.4%
- Property B – Cap Rate of 11.2%
- Property C – Cap rate of 9.8%

In this comparison, Property B would appear to be the one to analyze first, as the highest cap rate would suggest that it is a better investment than the other two. But let's think for a minute about how the cap rate would change if we were to purchase one of these properties and make changes:

1. We may find that one of them, maybe Property C, is charging below market rents that could be raised immediately, bringing up the cap rate.

2. We could find that Property B is a bit rundown because the owner has been cutting expenses by deferring maintenance, which would reduce the cap rate if we spend the money to maintain it properly.

3. We could find that the owner of Property A is a terrible manager and shopper, spending more than necessary on almost every expense line item. Simply by shopping

expenses better and lowering them, we could raise this cap rate significantly.

Once we have these cap rates, then we dig into the numbers for rents and expenses to see if there is an opportunity. It's possible that paying more for a property with a valid high cap rate is worth it. Or getting a bargain price on a lower cap rate that can be improved may be the way to go.

## Valuing a Property for Sale

The other use for cap rate is in valuing a property you own for sale. Here as a seller, you like a lower cap rate, and you do your market research and gather the cap rates for recently sold multi-family properties. You find that the prevailing average cap rate for well-maintained properties is 10.7% (.107). You want to see what you could sell your property for based on this number.

*Value/Sale Price = NOI / Cap Rate*

We're just moving the formula components around to make this happen. The possible selling price would be our NOI divided by that prevailing cap rate. So, if our property has NOI of $57,000, here's the calculation:

*Value/Sale Price = $57,000 / .107*

*Selling Price = $532,710*

Now we're going to look at it from the perspective that our property is very well-maintained, and we have really tight control of our expenses. We're also enjoying long occupancy cycles and a relatively low vacancy and credit loss number.

For these reasons, we believe that our property isn't "average," and we decide to move to the lower end of the cap rate spread. We find that one of the sold properties we evaluated sold with a cap rate of 9.8%, so we decide to use that, and our price is now $581,632 ($57,000 / .098). The savvy potential buyer will do the due diligence to see that our property may still be a good buy at a lower cap rate because of the other value factors.

Cap Rate is more detailed and a better picture of the value of a property, but you can see that it's still necessary to do more investigation, gather more information, and make a decision based on all of the facts.

## Spreadsheets for the Heavy Lifting

As I promised, I'm sharing a resource I found to help you do value analysis and to do these calculations for you. You can compare properties easily for both before and after tax returns. The two links are at the bottom of a short article about what they do, and you simply download and open them in Excel or your spreadsheet program. They are:

- A blank spreadsheet ready for your data entry, including links to calculation and entry explanations.
- The same spreadsheet with sample data entered so you can see results.

Get them here: http://realestate.about.com/b/2014/02/07/real-estate-investment-analysis-spreadsheets.htm.

## Perspectives & Progress

If you're math-challenged, don't worry. Most of these are really easy, and you should just practice with them using your own home and local sales data.

Try the spreadsheets, particularly if you are interested in larger or multi-family properties. These calculations are just one facet of a very comprehensive approach to value real estate investing. Which one you use will vary based on your investment strategy choices and experience level.

As an example, many of these will not be necessary if you're doing fix & flip. You'll be more involved in repair and renovation cost calculations, and the home value exercise in the next chapter. Just keep these in your investment toolbox for future reference.

---

### Chapter 9

# Calculate Home Values the Way The Pros Do It

*"Price is what you pay. Value is what you get." – Warren Buffett*

While Warren Buffett was talking about the stock market, the quote applies to just about anything bought and sold. The price people pay for something or what they're willing to sell it for can be a whole lot different from its actual value.

When valuing real estate as an investor, there are three values important to you: 1) market value, 2) value to your customer, usually another investor, and 3) value to you. Obviously, you'll be poor very quickly if you buy at market value and try to sell at a profit. Market value is what it is likely to sell for, so there's no room for profit in a deal like that. There's also no room for profit if you buy below market value but not far enough below to leave room to give the same benefit to your investor buyer.

All of this means that knowing how to properly determine three levels of value is critical to staying out of the poorhouse and being a successful real estate investor.

1.  What is the value in the retail marketplace of a home in livable condition? This is what a normal consumer buyer would pay for a home in which they want to live.

2.  What is the value to your rental property investor buyer who must be able to rent it out for a positive cash flow and will want to buy at some discount below current retail market value.

3.  What is the value to you once you have calculated what you'll need to invest between the purchase and the sale and still leave room for profit.

There's a lot of room for error in this three step valuation process, but you'll be confident about getting it right once you've read this book. We'll look at items 2 and 3 in future chapters about the strategies you'll be using. For now, we're going to learn how to calculate a home's retail market value the way that Realtors do it. They normally use what is called a CMA, Comparative Market Analysis.

## Why Not an Appraisal?

An appraiser has a very different job than the real estate agent. First, you should know that the appraiser is normally working for a lender. Their job is to conservatively value the home to cover the lender's risk. If you've bought and sold homes in the past, did you ever notice that almost all appraisals come in at the contract price or just slightly over? Why is that?

Since the vast majority of the business for an appraiser comes from lenders, there is no incentive for the appraiser to provide a value much in excess of the contract price, which they know before they do their job. Even if the buyer beats up a motivated seller and cuts a deal significantly below market value, the appraisal still seems to come in at the contract price or not far above it.

The appraiser has kept the deal alive with a contract price value, so the buyer gets their loan, and the lender isn't given a higher value that they may not be able to get in a foreclosure situation. The incentive is to not kill too many deals with low appraisals, and also not provide higher values that aren't necessary to make deals go through.

## The Real Estate Agent's Job is Different

The real estate agent is working with a homeowner who wants to sell for the most money they can get for their home. The real estate agent does the CMA with the goal of arriving at a list price that is at the top end of the expected realistic range. If there is demand, the home may sell quickly at that "best" price. If not, the price can be adjusted downward to generate buyer interest.

Some of the techniques used by appraisers are also used by real estate agents:

- They both gather "comps," comparable recently sold properties for their value calculations.

- They both make adjustments to the sold prices of those comps for differences in the homes.

But if you have a dozen available comps, which do you choose? Would you cherry pick the ones best suited to your objective? You may. The appraiser also has some very strict rules to go by since the real estate market crash. They must adjust a home's calculated value downward if the market statistics indicate a "declining" market. They also may use foreclosure sales in their valuation, which the real estate professional definitely would not do with a homeowner seller.

## The CMA, Comparative Market Analysis

When you want to determine the retail market value of a home as an investor, you'll rarely end up using the top end of the price range, as that doesn't suit your needs like it does the Realtor's. However, you can use the same process.

Do you need to learn this? Not if you find a real estate professional you trust to do the CMA for you. Keep in mind, though, that CMAs take some time to do so you may not be able to talk your Realtor into doing it. Even if you are working with an agent who shows you their CMA on a property, understanding the material here will allow you to decide if they used good comps and the right process. It's your business and your money.

There are four major components of a good CMA process, three of which are used by almost all real estate agents The fourth is not used as often.

1. **Location** – The comparable properties you select should be in the same neighborhood or a nearby neighborhood with similar style homes and price range. The nearer the better.

2. **Characteristics** – The homes should be as similar as possible, such as number of bedrooms, baths, garage type and spaces, etc. Age can be a problem if they're one home is much older. The idea is to make them as "comparable" as possible. You'll be adjusting for differences.

3. **When sold** – You want to use homes sold as recently in the past as possible, preferably within a month or two. You're already working with past data, and going too far back can result in errors due to changing markets.

4. **Adjust for the current market** – This has to do with the previous item, and this step is one many Realtors do not take. It's actually another CMA, but using currently listed properties and list prices. Markets can change rapidly, and homes get sold, removed from, and added to the market. Changes in supply and demand can change prices significantly and in a hurry. Getting another valuation based on the current market condition, especially if you've had to go back a few months for sold comps, is worthwhile.

## The CMA Process

### *Subject Property*

This is the home we want to value. Perhaps it's a home we're going to wholesale to a rental investor, or maybe it's one we will fix & flip. We'll talk about ARV, After Repair Value, later. You'll be valuing the home here as if it is in good condition and ready to occupy, no matter what its current condition.

We're going to run through an example, so let's set the characteristics of our subject property:

- **Location** – XYZ subdivision, a large subdivision with similar lot sizes throughout.
- **Characteristics**
  - 3 bedrooms
  - 2 baths
  - 1600 square feet
  - 2 car attached garage
  - 10 years old
  - No remodel or upgrades for age

It's important to understand that this isn't a precise science. A lot of decisions you'll make in valuation will be subjective, and there are a number of price adjustments you'll make based on property differences and their value. Don't stress out, as real estate professionals do this too, so you're not going to be far off from what they're telling their sellers. Three Realtors will almost always come up with three different CMA results.

## Comparable Property Selections

We've checked recently sold homes from MLS reports provided by a real estate agent resource. From these, we've selected three comparable properties.

### Comp A

This home is in the same subdivision and is close in age to our subject property, with these characteristics:

- 3 bedrooms
- 2.5 baths
- 2 car attached garage
- 1700 square feet
- Sold last month for $169,500

### Comp B

This home is in a neighboring subdivision nearby and similar in characteristics and price ranges. This whole area was built within a five year period, so no age adjustments need be made. Characteristics:

- 3 bedroom
- 2 bath
- Single car attached garage
- 1500 square feet
- Sold two weeks before for $146,000

## Comp C

This home is in the same subdivision as the subject property and is the same age. Characteristics:

- 2 bedroom
- 1.5 bath
- 1450 square feet
- Sold two months ago for $141,000

Those are our comparables, and now it's time to do some adjusting for the differences. We'll be changing those sold prices to bring the comps in line with the subject property's characteristics:

- Adding to the sold price if comp's characteristic are different to the downside (2 bedrooms instead of 3).

- Subtracting from the comparable's sold price for characteristics that exceed those of our subject property (more square footage).

What we're doing is saying that these comps would have sold for different prices, higher or lower, if they were exactly like our subject property.

How do we "adjust" the sold prices? This is where there's a lot of subjective decision-making. What is a half bath or an extra garage space worth? You can use the Internet to get some information, but don't use remodel estimates. It's a lot less expensive to add an extra bathroom when a home is being built than to add it later.

One great way to get this info is to ask an appraiser to help you.

They're doing exactly the same thing, so they have values for these features and characteristics. Set up a chart with what you'll use as the value of a bedroom, bath, half bath, garage space, etc.

### Comp A Adjustments

This home has an extra half bath and 100 square feet more than our subject property. Assuming that those features contributed to the higher selling price, we will be subtracting the value of those items from that price.

- The square footage is easy. Divide the sold price by the number of square feet to get a dollar amount per square foot. Then multiply by 100 and subtract from the sold price. *$169,500 / 1700 = $99.71 X 100 = $9971. Subtract from the sold price to get adjusted sold price of $159,529.*

- For the half bath, our appraiser friend tells us that it's worth an extra $3800. Taking our adjusted sold price, we adjust it again. *$159,529 - $3800 = $155,729 as our new adjusted sold price.*

### Comp B Adjustments

This home is 100 square feet smaller and has a single car garage. Both are less than our subject property, so we'll be adding to this sold price to make the homes more comparable.

- *$146,000 / 1500 X 100 = $9,733. New sold = $155,733.*
- Appraiser says attached garages are valued at $9,000 per space. *New sold raised to $164,733.*

### Comp C Adjustments

This home is smaller, has only two bedrooms and 1.5 baths instead of two, so we'll be adding to the sold price for these differences.

- *$141,000 / 1450 X 150 = $14,586. New sold = $155,586.*
- *$155,586 + $3800 (half bath) = new sold of $159,386.*

That wasn't so hard was it? The hardest work is up front in establishing values for characteristics. OK, let's see our new sold prices:

- Comp A = $155,729
- Comp B = $164,733
- Comp C = $159,386

Now it's time to apply these to the valuation of our subject property. Since we've already adjusted the three comps for the difference in square footage, we just divide these three numbers by 1600 (subject property) and average the result.

$$\$155,729 / 1600 = \$97.33 \text{ per sq foot}$$
$$\$164,733 / 1600 = \$102.95 \text{ per sq foot}$$
$$\$159,386 / 1600 = \$99.62 \text{ per sq foot}$$
$$\$97.33 + \$102.95 + \$99.62 = \$299.90$$
$$\$299.90 / 3 = \$99.97/\text{sq foot average}$$

Now we multiply that by 1600 to get our subject property's value:

*$159,952*

You can see that a number of decisions and estimated values go into a CMA calculation, so don't get stressed out worrying you've made a world-ending error. This number could be the one you want to use, or you may want to raise or lower it based on the current market. This is where the second CMA comes in.

If you suspect that there has been a significant change in available home inventory or demand, or if your comps were a little old, you may want to go through the process again. This time use the list prices for comps currently on the market. If there has been a significant change, you can adjust the first number up or down.

Now that you know the current market value of the home, you can do your other calculations to see what you're willing to pay for it to make a profit and resell it to an investor, or you may be keeping it as a rental. We'll get to those calculations later.

---

### Perspectives & Progress

Whether you intend to do these or get help from a Realtor, you should understand how they work so you can check their results and make sure they made good comp selections.

Use your own home or a neighbor's, get comparable sales from the MLS (from a real estate agent if necessary), and do some practice runs through the adjustments. It doesn't matter which strategy you choose for profits in your business, you will need to have an accurate market value for the home.

### Chapter 10

# *A Hobby is for Fun*
# *A Business is for Profit*

*"I have an expensive hobby: buying homes, redoing them, tearing them down and building them up the way they want to be built. I want to be an architect." – Sandra Bullock*

Sandra Bullock is at least admitting that her house projects are a hobby and cost a lot of money. That's a hobby. You're about to be a business ... which is a big difference. You can play dominoes as a hobby, but you'll want to line up your dominoes properly in your real estate investment business. If you don't, you're likely to get one of those chain reactions, only it will be money that's crashing.

Right now you should be digging into the structure of your business, including legal matters, tax considerations, liability, and more. It's not as difficult as you may think. However, don't do it without expert advice. Consult a CPA and an attorney.

## Choose Your Business Structure

The business structure you choose will have legal and tax implications. Learn about the different types of business structures and find the one best suited for your business.

 ARTICLE

**Sole Proprietorship**

A sole proprietorship is the most basic type of business to establish. You alone own the company and are responsible for its assets and liabilities. Learn more about the sole proprietor structure.

 ARTICLE

**Limited Liability Company**

An LLC is designed to provide the limited liability features of a corporation and the tax efficiencies and operational flexibility of a partnership. Learn more about how LLCs are structured.

ARTICLE

**Cooperative**

People form cooperatives to meet a collective need or to provide a service that benefits all member-owners. Learn more about how cooperatives are structured.

 ARTICLE

**Corporation**

A corporation is more complex and generally suggested for larger, established companies with multiple employees. Learn more about how Corporations are structured.

ARTICLE

**Partnership**

There are several different types of partnerships, which depend on the nature of the arrangement and partner responsibility for the business. Learn more about how these are structured.

ARTICLE

**S Corporation**

An S corporation is similar to a C corporation but you are taxed only on the personal level. Learn more about how S corporations are structured.

There are tax and legal considerations in forming a business that can be difficult and expensive to change later. The image is from the SBA.gov website, and there is some helpful information there.

## Legal and Liability

In this chapter I'm not going to go into detail about business structures or corporate formation. Those are explanations that should come from your attorney and accountant. But this chapter is to remind you of the things you need to think about early in your new business.

You'll want to protect yourself and your assets from legal action, even though it's probable you'll never do anything to warrant a lawsuit. In this country people can sue for any reason, so it can come out of the blue, be totally unwarranted, and yet cost you a bundle to defend.

If you invest in rental properties, you definitely need to work with an attorney. There are off-the-shelf leases and other forms used in rental property management, and there may be some specifically for your state laws. However, you still need to have them blessed by your attorney and modified as necessary to protect your interests. Landlord-tenant laws get stricter every year, and it's easy to do or say something that can get you into trouble and cost you money.

The buying and investment decisions you will be making after you finish reading this book may have legal consequences. Sit down now, consult with experts, and form your business in the most beneficial structure from both legal and tax perspectives.

## Accounting and Taxes

This is a major consideration, and it should be balanced with the legal aspect. It's not easy to change your business structure later if you find you're paying more in taxes than you should be. Sometimes it's impossible, and usually doesn't back up to previous deals.

As you read this book and begin to plan for the investing strategies you want to use, meet with your accountant and discuss them and the tax considerations. The tax advantages available to real estate investors are a major benefit of the business, but there are different ways to go about your dealings that influence the taxes you'll pay.

Don't limit your discussion to the strategies you like today. You may just find that as your business grows you'll want to do more. You may think that wholesaling is your thing, but a couple of years from now you may want to buy rental properties. The money you'll pay your accountant for an hour or so of discussion could save you tens of thousands of dollars later.

## Overhead, Facilities & Equipment

This is another area where we find that real estate investing is a great business. You can start with almost nothing, working at your kitchen table or in your home office. There are a couple of things you really should have, but most of us already do:

- **Smartphone** – You'll be communicating with many different people, from contractors to real estate agents, and buyers and sellers. You want to be available at all times so you don't miss an opportunity. The many great apps you can get today will let your phone take the place of other gadgets. You can use it as a GPS, a map, a portable filing cabinet, and a great calendar and task management tool.

- **Computer & Internet** – At home or in your office, you'll extend your capabilities for market research and communications via email with a computer. Whether it's a desktop, notebook, or even a tablet computer, you'll want a keyboard for speedy input. You will be writing letters and doing spreadsheets, so make sure you have *Microsoft*, *Apple*, or *Open Office* applications.

- **Chair, desk, file cabinet** – This pretty much makes up your office, and the kitchen table can be the desk at first. The file cabinet can be smaller if you use databases and other tools like Evernote to decrease the number of paper documents you need to keep.

Working in the "Cloud," some investors start out with only their phone and work from coffee shops with computers and WiFi. Check out Google products for a cloud solution that's free and combines multiple features and tools all stored in the cloud:

- *Gmail* for email.
- *Google Docs* for word processing and spreadsheets.
- *Google Drive* for storage of documents and photos in the cloud.

These tools will allow you to be completely mobile, while still having access to your tools and files from anywhere with Web access or on your cell phone. There are even apps for iPhone and Android that provide word processing and spreadsheet software and save them to Google Drive. Add a portable Bluetooth keyboard and you're in business.

The image below is of an Apple Bluetooth keyboard in a case that opens and folds back to the right angle to support a tablet or phone. It's easy and fast to set up and very portable. The Apple keyboard is a good choice because it runs on AA batteries, so the recharging hassle is avoided. It's also almost full size like your computer keyboard. The image is the *OfficeSuite* app on the phone.

With one of these keyboards, a smart phone, and the right apps, you can do almost everything on the go:

- Word processing
- Spreadsheets
- Mortgage calculations
- Photo editing
- Bookkeeping
- Note taking
- Calendar management
- Post a WordPress blog/website
- More

There are very few businesses you can start up with almost upfront cash, zero overhead, and totally mobile operations. It's great to be a real estate investor!

## The Business Needs a Boss

This is important. It's true that when you are starting out you're not going to be an expert. You'll be relying on some help from your team, and we'll talk about the team in the next chapter. But, you own your business, you're the boss, and you should make the decisions.

This is especially true when you're working with real estate professionals. When you hear "this house is a steal," check your pockets. As you gain experience, you'll recognize a deal, and you'll also end up with trusted real estate agents on your team who will understand your business and not be "selling" you on properties.

If you're doing fix & flip, you must take charge of your contractors and repair people. As you grow, you may partner with some of them in projects, giving them more authority to make decisions, buy materials, or hire subs. But never forget that you're the boss, it's your money at risk, and the ultimate decisions are yours to make.

## Perspectives & Progress

This is the time to begin discussions with your current accountant or spend some time to locate a good one. We'll talk about it in the team chapter next. It's time to begin researching local attorneys. In some states there are registered specializations, and real estate would be one. In others, there is no formal designation, but you'll find that there will be attorneys who specialize in real estate law. You definitely want this, as it's not the same as injury, divorce, or general business law.

### Chapter 11

# *Effective Outsourcing:*
# *Building Your Investment Group*

*"I've always found that the speed of the boss is the speed of the team."*
*– Lee Iacocca*

There's a lot of information out there about building an investment team. These are the other people involved in your success who provide services you need to get the job done and to manage and grow your business. While the word "team" works, you're really outsourcing, and not everyone has a common goal like a team wanting to win the game. It's one game, and they all want the same thing.

Lee Iacocca's quote is a good one, as you really set the pace of your investment group. They don't all have a single common goal. Sure, most of them are concerned with your success for repeat business, but they each have their own primary goal and motivation:

- Real estate agents – the commission.
- Contractors – a profitable job completion.
- Attorneys and accountants – their fees.
- Title companies – sell title insurance.
- Lenders – acceptable risk & loan profits

You are the ONLY one involved who has the single goal of your profit and growing your business. They can all want to see you succeed, but only within the limitations of their individual business goals. Later, if your business gets really large, you may partner with some of them or even hire them as employees. Then they would have more of a common goal with you.

For most of us, though, we may end up changing relationships often, especially with lenders, title companies, real estate agents, and contractors. The pace of the group will be ours to set, and we need to understand our role and make the hard choices and steer the group.

## Your Pace is What You Want it to Be

Another great thing about the real estate investment business is that you can keep it as small or grow it as large as your dreams. You can set the pace of that growth, and you should. Too fast and you may outgrow your funding, which is not a good thing. Too slow, and you may not reach your ultimate retirement objectives. A major component of growth is outsourcing things you can't or don't have time to do, those you don't want to do, and those things others can do better.

As you go through these short comments on the potential members of your investment group, remember that you may need only a couple people right now and maybe only a few this coming year. You may never need all of them. It depends on your investment strategies and how much you want to delegate to others. This is your business, and it will run the way you design it to run. Let's get on with a quick overview of the people involved.

### *Accountant and Attorney*

We've already talked about these two professionals. Take your time, do some research, ask trusted people for recommendations, check references, and look for real estate specific knowledge and experience.

Your accountant will end up being a long-term partner in your success. They know that giving you poor advice this year is going to show up in next year's taxes. They want to keep you as a client and grow their fees as your business grows. You may use an accountant now who may not be the best choice for real estate. Make sure that they have other investor clients or specialize in this business.

The attorney you select is going to be a sporadic resource; at least you hope you won't need them often. However, any new documents you'll be using frequently, like leases or disclosures, should be run by the attorney. In many states the contracts used by Realtors are state-mandated, and they're set up by a team of real estate brokers and attorneys to be fair to both sides. In most cases, they'll work for you, but you don't always want to be fair to both sides, especially when you're one of them. A rental property lease is an example. You'll want to have one written that is legal but more in your interests than those of the tenant. Search for real estate specialists.

### Real Estate Agents

The most important thing to remember about this group is that on the whole they spend less than 90-120 hours in training before they take an exam. They aren't experts at much of anything when they get their license. Some can become experts, and some can be excellent resources. But too many are in the business because they perceive it to be easy money. That's why during down periods the number of licensees falls off dramatically. They can't hold on with low skill sets.

It takes a special type of real estate professional to work with an active investor. First, they can't do their customary "selling" of properties that might generally work with consumers. Showing the cook the kitchen and the mechanic the garage isn't going to work with the real estate investor.

The agent also needs to understand our business and the ways in which we profit from it. They may be making many offers, with only a few going through to closing. So an efficient agent who uses today's technology tools to make this process easier will be more likely to stick with you.

Don't go to the Web and check out reviews, as too many are solicited from consumer customers who say what the agent tells them to say. Ask other investors or lenders which agents tend to work most with investors. Finally, when you have a short list, call their office and ask whoever answers the phone for the agent who works most with investors. See who they put on the phone, and ask a lot of questions about deals they've done with investor clients.

### Mortgage Brokers & Transaction Lenders

We'll talk about transactional funding later, but know that it's just borrowing short-term money to fund deals. So, we group them with mortgage brokers because we're generally looking for money from both of them.

Mortgage brokers work mostly with consumers, but there are some who welcome investors and their different needs. Get recommendations from other investors, and see which brokers are members of investment clubs. They're seeking out investor business.

We don't always want to borrow funds. However, If we end up flipping houses to consumers at retail or rental property investors, they will need funding for their purchase. A good relationship with an aggressive mortgage broker can make your sale easier and maybe for more money by hooking them up with your buyer.

Transaction lenders specialize in working with investors. They provide short-term money for wholesale and fix & flip deals. We'll get into more detail later, but a good relationship with this group can make you a lot of money.

### Title & Abstract Companies

Many times you have no control over where a deal will close, as the other party may make that selection. However, when you do have the choice, work with a title company that's efficient, doesn't make mistakes, and helps you with information when you need it.

You may need a quick printout of liens or documents recorded about a property you're considering buying. In today's computerized world, often a good title company can print one out while you wait. It can save a lot of legwork if you see there are liens or problems with title on a home.

Title companies are also contacted by owners who want to sell. In many cases, they're asking questions about selling because they want to avoid real estate commissions. They may own their homes outright as well. A good relationship could get you referred as a potential buyer or wholesaler.

### *Contractors*

This is a group that can make or break profits on a fix & flip deal. They're also important if you own rental properties, as repair expenses eat away at cash flow. There is a lot more research necessary in selecting members of this group.

Get recommendations, ALWAYS ask for references, and check their work and customer satisfaction. A low bid should not be your primary objective, especially in renovation work. Their ability to stay on schedule, coordinate their subcontractors, and stay within budget is much more important.

Always work toward at least two or more in each category:

- General contractors
- Electricians
- Plumbers
- Flooring
- Carpentry
- Cabinetry
- Swimming pools and hot tubs
- Roofing
- Painters

We'll get into more detail in the fix & flip chapters, but the basics of adding this group to your team involve reliability, performance, quality, and then price.

### *Property Management*

Until you get into rental property investing and own several, you'll likely handle your own management. But at some point it's going to stunt your business growth if you don't hire out this function. Get recommendations from other rental investors. As most states require a real estate license for this activity, check their disciplinary record with the state real estate board.

Most property management firms give you some choices as to the level of their services which will change the cost. You want to be sure that there is a clear understanding of how they will handle tenant acquisition, interviews, leasing, and rent collection. You don't want to use a company that is going to get you into legal trouble.

## Get Them When You Need Them

Starting out, you may not need to spend much time researching or selecting team players. One good practice is to begin to take notice of professionals in these groups as you meet them in the course of business. Make notes about their performance and keep them in mind for the future. You may find that when you have the need, you already have the information necessary for a selection.

---

## Perspectives & Progress

If this seems like information overload because you're not even sure what you'll be doing and which strategies you'll use, that's OK. It is information you will need, so just keep it stored away until you do.

The first steps should be with an attorney and accountant, as you'll want to start out right with your business structure. Start now to build relationships with real estate agents and to get them to feed you information such as sold property and new listing reports. Just let the rest ride until you make some strategy decisions.

### Chapter 12

## *Profit by Adding Value to Each Investment Strategy*

*"We get paid by bringing value to the marketplace." – Jim Rohn*

Unless we're buying for our own rental property portfolio, we're the middle person between buyers and sellers. We didn't place ourselves there. If a buyer and seller find each other and can make a deal, they will. We end up in the middle because of the value we bring to the table.

It's a great business because we have a chance to add value to both sides. There are motivated sellers who haven't been able to sell for various reasons, or there are homeowners in trouble who have no idea what to do. The third group is full of lenders with foreclosure properties they need to get off the books.

On the buyer side, we're normally going to have rental investors for customers. But there's a growing market for more upscale fix & flip investors selling to retail customers. Depending on the strategy and how you structure your business, you have choices. But you don't have a choice as to how you make money ... it is only by bringing added value to the transactions.

The puzzle image is a good one because we can think of business as a puzzle needing all of the pieces in place before money is made or properties sold. Our goal and profit opportunity is to fill in the missing piece in the business plan. Let's get an overview of how we add value in each of the primary investment strategies in this book so you can begin to plan the strategies you want to use. We'll have detailed chapters on each later.

## The Bird Dog

This is an entry level strategy that helps some investors get their feet wet and make some money while they learn the market and skills to use in other strategies. The bird dog is someone who locates potential deals for investors and brings them to their attention.

As a bird dog you're not buying, selling, or signing any contracts. You're just locating homes that may be right for investors and letting them know about them. It doesn't require any money, just transportation and the ability to recognize what could be a good deal. We'll get into detail later.

*Value Added: Depending on your skills and efforts, you find houses that are abandoned, or you locate distressed owners. You turn over the address and what you know to an investor, and you're paid some pre-agreed fee for doing so. How much depends on the arrangement. Sometimes you'll get a small cash payment for each lead, but more often you'll be paid more when the deal actually closes.*

## Wholesaling by Assignment

As a wholesaler, you locate what you know is a good deal for one or more investors on your buyer list. Using an assignment contract we'll explain later, you need only put up a small amount of earnest money, and you then assign your contract rights to the buyer. The buyer then takes over all of your rights and obligations and takes the deal to closing. You're normally paid at closing.

*Value Added: You're adding more value here, and you'll make more money. You not only have the skill to locate opportunities, but you can value the home in the current market, negotiate a bargain price with the owner, and contract to buy. The seller gets the value of your buyer contacts and your negotiations to move their property. Your buyer sees the first value component as you having control so they need to deal with you. The second value component is your skill at negotiating a deal the buyer wants with some profit in it for you.*

## Wholesaling by Buying

This is a higher level strategy, and it requires more skill on your part, as well as some financing arrangements. You're doing the same thing as you do in assignment wholesaling, except now you're going through with the purchase transaction and immediately selling to your investor buyer. You make more money, as you're presenting a selling price independent of what you paid. The better the deal you cut on the buying side, the more profit you make on the sale.

*Value Added: It's pretty much the same as assignment wholesaling, except you are bringing a cleaner deal to the buyer. They don't have to go through as much due diligence as taking over an assignment. A major value component in both of these wholesale strategies is your ability to locate and lock up deals your investor buyers are unable to find on their own.*

## Fix & Flip to Investor Buyer

Much of your fix & flip activity, if not all of it, will be locating distressed homes, renovating/rehabbing them, and then selling them to rental property investors. By building up your buyer list with active investors, you will know what they want and where they want it. You locate properties that are not in sellable condition, and you do the work to get them ready for sale.

*Value Added: You're adding the greatest value of all of the strategies in fix & flip.*

- *Your skills at locating properties and negotiating deep enough discounts to rehab them and sell at a discount under market value to rental investors.*
- *Your market knowledge and valuation ability in determining an accurate ARV, After Repair Value, as well as knowing*

*the rental market and what your buyers can get for rent on the home.*

- *Your project management and negotiation skills in working with suppliers and contractors to get the work done on time and under budget.*
- *Knowing what your investors want and what they're willing to pay, and delivering it on a silver platter.*

As foreclosure inventories shrink, a higher percentage of available properties are in poor condition. Since so many rental investors are only interested in a ready-to-rent property, this opens up opportunities.

## Fix & Flip to Retail Buyers

In this strategy, you're adding a real estate agent and some marketing to the mix. You're going to make higher margins on these deals, as you're dealing with consumers buying more with emotion than with the cold calculations investors use. Materials are of higher quality, finishes are nicer, and selling prices can be retail at higher margins.

There are actually two markets here. One is the price-conscious value buyer. Your homes will be in the lower price ranges with less fancy features and finishes. The other is in up-scale markets and price ranges. You can get higher margins on higher priced homes.

**Value Added:** *All of the value adds in rental investor buyer flips apply here as well, but with one more value add. You're providing homes for buyers in areas where they may not be able to find ready homes. You're also able to choose homes in just the right areas where there is demand but low or no inventory. A buyer may really want to buy a certain home, but because of condition, they can't get a mortgage. You solve that problem for them.*

From here forward, we'll be getting into detailed instructions about each of these strategies and how to profit from each in your business. We'll talk about negotiations for foreclosures, short sales, and distressed owner-occupied homes.

## Perspectives & Progress

This is your introduction to the strategies, so begin to think about which may be of interest. Don't let money enter into your process now, as funding is out there.

These are all buying and selling strategies, but rental property investing is the long-term wealth-building strategy. Financing is a little more involved, as you'll need mortgages, but we'll get into that in detail, too.

For now, go back over the value you add in each of this chapter's strategies. If we don't bring added value to the table, we won't be sitting there.

*Chapter 13*

---

## *Foreclosure Fortunes*

*"Foreclosure is to no one's benefit. I've heard estimates that mortgage investors lose 40 to 50 percent on their investment if it goes into foreclosure." – Henry Paulson*

The quote is from Henry Paulson in his position as the Secretary of the Treasury. It's not wholly accurate simply because he is referring to losses incurred only by the banks, mortgage lenders, and their underwriters. Of course, the homeowners lost the most.

But saying everyone loses is incorrect, because tens of thousands of small investors and dozens of institutional and big investment conglomerates are making a ton of money off of foreclosures. There's a whole chain of investors involved in wholesaling, renovating, flipping, and renting out foreclosure properties. Investors should get more credit for helping to alleviate the pain of many homeowners by throwing them a life preserver before foreclosure through short sales help and outright cash purchases.

This chapter isn't about specific investment strategies, as we'll dig into those in detail later. Here I want to give you some basic information about how foreclosures work, as well as motivations and tactics used by the lenders.

## Types of Foreclosure

There are two main classifications of foreclosures that are based on whether a court must be involved or not. They are a matter of state law.

### *Judicial Foreclosure*

Judicial foreclosures must go through a court process. Of course this makes them more expensive and time-consuming than others. There are currently 20 states requiring only judicial foreclosure and another few states using it primarily. Some others have a mix of judicial and non-judicial, and others are on a case-by-case basis due to verbiage in the mortgage.

States with only judicial foreclosure can see lags of a year or more to move a home through the foreclosure process. After the media attention on the robo-signing court cases and settlements, courts and attorneys are examining the documents tracing ownership much more carefully. This has increased the duration of foreclosure proceedings in those states. The normal steps in a judicial foreclosure are:

1. **Date of Default** – Under the terms of the mortgage, this is the date the borrower is considered in default on the loan. This and the period prior when late notices are being sent out is considered the pre-foreclosure period.

2. **In Foreclosure**
   a. **Initiation** – the borrower's information is referred to the foreclosure attorney.
   b. **Filing** – the attorney files a complaint in court to seek foreclosure.
   c. **Court Approval** – the date the court officially approves

the process to move forward after reviewing documentation.

    d. **Transfer Date** – the date the transfer of ownership is completed to the highest bidder or to the lender as a Bank Owned property.

3. **Post Foreclosure** – If they are still in the home, the owner is evicted. The home is then marketed by the lender, usually through a real estate broker.

The steps involved are expensive and lengthy, so some homeowners can enjoy months to a year or more of free rent while this process moves forward.

### *Non-judicial Foreclosure*

Non-judicial foreclosure states use a deed of trust, and the trustee holding the deed usually can initiate and handle the foreclosure process. It's faster and less expensive. Some states only allow trustee sales, while many others involve other parties, but it's still a faster and less expensive process than judicial foreclosure.

The steps in this process are fewer and quicker:

1. A notice of default is mailed when the period prescribed in the mortgage is reached without full payment of mortgage payments and penalties.

2. A short period of time, usually 30 to 60 days, is allowed for the homeowner to bring their mortgage to current status by paying all late payments and penalties.

3. If that does not happen, a notice of sale date is filed with the courthouse, mailed to the homeowner, and published publicly. The sale is made and the homeowner evicted.

Check your state's laws and documentation requirements for foreclosure to see how they're handled. For our investment purposes, we're usually not too concerned with how the foreclosure came to market, just that it has. However, in extreme cases, there have been purchases nullified by the courts due to poor documentation by the lenders that comes out later in a court action.

## Motivations of the Parties Involved

Let's take a look at who is involved in a foreclosure and their motivations and concerns so that we understand how sales and the prices at which they close come about.

### *The Investor Buyer*

This is us, so it's an easy one. We're in the market to buy a fore-closure that fits into our investing strategy and will yield a profit in either the short or long term.

- Wholesalers usually want to flip the property to another investor without having to do any rehab. We're looking for a deep discount that will allow us to pass it along at a profit, but still at a discount to value that will appeal to our investor buyer.

- Fix & Flip investors want to buy foreclosures in need of work, do the rehab and repairs, and then sell them either on the retail market or, more likely, to a rental property investor. Sometimes the worse the condition, the better the deal, and the more value added and profit received by the investor.

- Rental property investors generally will want a foreclosure in ready-to-rent condition, or one that needs only cosmetic and inexpensive repairs. They want to get a tenant into the property as soon as possible.

Foreclosure homes have made fortunes for smart investors over the past few years, and they still are. As inventories shrink, however, the foreclosure buyer needs to sharpen their pencil and improve their strategy, cost structure, and buyer list in order to continue to make the good money.

### *The Bank or Lender*

It's easy to think that the primary or sole motivation of the bank is to get the property sold as soon as possible to get it off the books. Unfortunately, what you see in real life can make you wonder if they're smoking something in the boardroom.

To a certain point, their government guaranteed mortgages are providing some reimbursement for loss. However, once the sale price drops below a certain point, it's a real loss on the books. As investor buyers, we don't know what dollar amount is at that bottom line. When you make a discounted offer on a foreclosure property, especially after one or more price reductions, they may keep coming back with full list price counter offers. Obviously, you're at that bottom line, and they're willing to wait for a better offer.

You're often not even dealing with the lender. You're dealing with a third party asset management company. They have their instructions from the lender, and they're not going to budge once they hit a certain price point without getting new instructions.

After saying all of that, here's the thing to do: ALWAYS make a low offer, lower than even their recently discounted list price! Unlike a homeowner of 20 years or a young couple selling their love nest, you can't offend a bank or asset manager. They have a sort of loan assembly line, and they will just reject or counter offer when you don't fit into their plan.

We don't know the numbers and boardroom discussions involved in a bank-owned property sale. For this reason, we should be making low offers on every property that may meet our needs. A counter offer or rejection is just a tactic. You may be able to wait them out, or you may lose the property. Either way, you know your bottom line number, so stick to it.

### *The Real Estate Agent*

The simple motivation here is for a commission. However, there are also some burdens placed on the agent that make listing foreclosures a real hassle. Generally, they'll be happy to present any offer that may lead to a closing and allow them to get rid of a headache. Often they're managing the property at their expense and awaiting reimbursement for items like security, necessary repairs for sale, utilities payments, and more. Rarely do you need to be concerned that an agent will have a problem with a low offer because their commission will go down, as they're usually working on a discounted commission structure with the lender anyway.

## The Closing Process

If you ever watched the old TV series Hogan's Heroes, you remember Sergeant Schultz. He was the prisoner camp guard whose favorite sayings were, "I know nothing," or, "I see nothing," a lot like the three monkeys who don't see, speak, or hear any evil.

This is what you experience when it comes to seller disclosures in a foreclosure closing. The bank knows nothing, and they're going to say that no matter what. They want:

- NO responsibility for problems with encroachments or any title issue that need not be corrected to close the sale.
- NO responsibility for repairs or property condition problems.
- NO responsibility for homeowner association covenants or other restrictions or you may not like.
- NO responsibility for guaranteeing any property rights that aren't necessary to close the deal. An example would be water rights or an easement.
- NO responsibility for ANYTHING that they can possibly avoid and still get the deal closed.

Basically, go into a foreclosure purchase with the knowledge that you're buying what you see at the agreed upon price, and pretty much you're on your own after that. For this reason, be sure that someone with the right expertise has inspected the property for major defects that would ruin your investment plan.

Just to clarify how frustrating it can be, a transaction comes to mind where a major bank owned a foreclosure property, and another branch of the same bank in a different city was doing the financing for the buyer. The two branches of the same bank refused to discuss with each other even the most minor issues, one being a difference in the spelling of the street name in one deed in the chain of title. It took four months to close the deal, with infighting between the two branches every step of the way.

That is an extreme example, but illustrates how you need to mentally approach a foreclosure purchase. A cash purchase is definitely less of a hassle, as you don't have another lender throwing their requirements into the mix. If you enter the deal with the expectation of getting only what you see for the purchase price, you'll be pleasantly surprised if you get a concession along the way.

## Sources for Foreclosure Information

You shouldn't wait for a foreclosure property to come out in the local Multiple Listing Service to get a jump on the competition. There are other resources.

### *The BPO & Foreclosure Listing Agents*

There are going to be many real estate professionals in your area who do not want the hassles of foreclosure listings. This usually causes a concentration of foreclosure listings with a few very active agents. Check the local foreclosure listings to see which top two or three agents have the most listings. Contact them to build a relationship. They love investor buyers who can help them move these listings. There can be days to weeks between them first knowing that they're going to list a property until they've done photos and document retrieval to get the listing out there. You can be doing your due diligence early.

A BPO is a Broker Price Opinion. This is an even earlier alert to a probable foreclosure. When a homeowner is going into default, agencies hired by the lenders will have a list of local real estate professionals willing to do a price opinion on a property either by driving by or getting access.

They're normally paid a nominal flat fee, perhaps $50 to $100 depending on what they have to do. They always have a detailed form to fill out about the condition of the property and other factors influencing the value they report. It's like a mini-CMA.

- **Drive-by BPO** – The lender doesn't want a confrontation with a homeowner who is late on their payments, so they get a drive-by opinion, with the agent trying to see as much of the exterior of the property, front and back, as possible.

- **Interior BPO** – The lender either has permission from the homeowner for a visit or they believe the property to be abandoned. This is a much more thorough BPO, more like a full CMA.

Many agents who do these are not expecting to get the listing, and are just hard up for some income. But this makes them a great early warning system for you. If you can get to know some of them, you'll know about foreclosures sometimes months in advance. You may even see an opportunity to try a strategy to get the home before foreclosure is initiated.

### *Foreclosure Websites*

These are sites that publish information about homes either in foreclosure or on which default notices have been filed. The largest and most used is *RealtyTrac.com*. You may be able to see the amount due on the mortgage to gauge the opportunity.

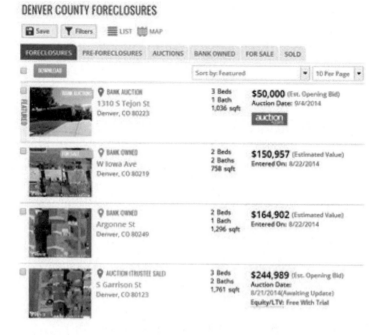

RealtyTrac.com is a good resource for watching the local fore-closure market as a whole.

---

## Perspectives & Progress

Begin to watch the local foreclosure inventory, both in the MLS and online sites. Identify active foreclosure listing agents. Start asking agents if they do BPOs. Build a resource list and keep in touch for advance information.

Foreclosure buying is a competitive business, so any advance notice you can get will allow you to do your due diligence early. Having more time will also help you to avoid costly errors from hurried valuations and property inspections.

---

### Chapter 14

# Short Sales:
# Less Competition but More Work

*"A 'For Sale' sign in your yard during the holidays is like a 'kick me' sign.*
*You are telling buyers you are a distressed seller." – Ray Brown*

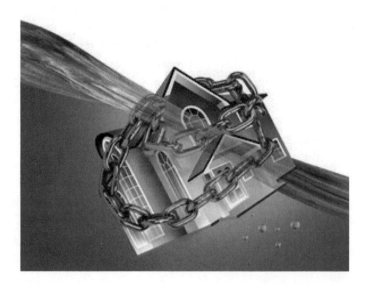

A short sale is the sale of a home with the lender accepting less than the amount owed on the mortgage ("short" of the mortgage payoff amount). The quote in this chapter isn't about short sales specifically, but it does illustrate the homeowner's situation well.

A short sale is being considered because the homeowner is behind on payments, owes more on the mortgage than the home is worth, and would like to avoid foreclosure. The "kick me" part comes from the bank/lender being in a position to kick the home-owner around depending on the situation. A short comment on the history of short sales can help us to understand what's happening in a short sale negotiation in current markets.

Starting in 2007 and going through 2010 and 2011, the banks

were processing foreclosures as fast as their staff and procedures allowed. They were set up for this, though not for the volume. Foreclosure is a process that they know well and for which they have well-defined procedures. Short sales were a different kettle of fish.

Assembly lines for foreclosures were in place, but not for short sales. Because of this, for a long time short sale offers were very difficult to get to the closing table. Months would pass with the homeowner and an investor making their offer, waiting, sending required documents, waiting, sending the documents again, and waiting…

At one point only around 25% of short sale offers were making it to the closing table because buyers gave up and pulled their offers. It wasn't just that the lenders weren't set up for them; they just seemed to want to go to foreclosure because it was perceived to be faster and less expensive. In many cases it seemed to be an attitude that giving in to a homeowner and letting them out of the mortgage with a shortfall wasn't good for the lender.

As the foreclosure pipeline slowed down a bit, and probably because there was enough history to understand what foreclosures were costing the lenders, short sales gained in favor. One probable reason was that the homeowner was still in the home, wanting to get the deal done, and the home was still in pretty good or excellent condition.

Letting them go to foreclosure frequently resulted in a vacant and even vandalized home in very poor condition. Some homeowners were stripping everything of value before moving out. Many homes ended up without plumbing and wiring. It was no longer just comparing the time it took to resolve the situation or the legal costs. The discounts at sale were much higher for damaged homes in need of complete rehab.

Starting in 2011, many lenders realized the trade-offs, and they began to not only look more kindly on short sales, but also to encourage them. Some banks even began to send out letters to homeowners in trouble encouraging them to search for a short sale buyer, and in some cases even pre-approving short sales.

Bank of America went even further, offering cash incentives to homeowners in some areas. Letters went out offering $5,000 to $20,000 according to some reports. Wells Fargo, JP Morgan Chase, and Citibank had similar programs. Even if a short sale deal wasn't offered, the processing of short sales got faster and easier. The lenders saw significant cost and time savings by avoiding the foreclosure process.

All of this doesn't mean that it's a slam dunk to get a short sale through to closing. The banks still balance the offer, market conditions, and cost of a foreclosure to make decisions. And, though faster, it's still a drawn out process. This is why there is less competition among investors for homes that may be short sale opportunities.

## The Short Sale Process

Let's take a look at how the process works, what you as an investor need to do to help the homeowner, and strategies that may help.

### Connecting with Homeowners in Trouble

Refer back to the marketing chapter and consider the type of classified and Craigslist ads you can run. Think about social media and try to locate discussions about foreclosure and short sales. Create a small website focused just on short sale to avoid foreclosure. It can be as small as one of those single page sales sites you've seen.

It's really important to understand your role and the fact that you're offering a valuable service to troubled homeowners. Sure, you'll make money, but you're helping them a lot as well. They are in trouble with missed payments and maybe a default notice in hand. You want to catch them before a notice of sale to give you time to work the deal.

### Short Sale Requirements

Look for a set of circumstances and mortgage details that will be most likely to result in a successful short sale at a price that works with your investment strategy. Short sales can be great opportunities if you're buying a rental property for yourself or flipping to a rental investor. You create the deal for them because they couldn't have found it elsewhere. The other advantage for a rental unit is that the property should be in ready-to-rent condition, needing only cosmetic repairs if any. Other requirements include:

- An "upside down" homeowner who owes more on the home than they can get in a normal sale.
- Clear title, without any large liens that would be a hit on your profits to clear.
- Time to complete the process; if they already have a sale notice, it's probably too late.
- A willing and helpful seller. You shouldn't have to convince them; they should jump at the opportunity.
- The numbers have to work. Do your valuation CMA, including any ARV, After Repair Value, calculations. Considering the mortgage balance, there must be a realistic chance to get the deal done at a profit.
- Verifiable homeowner hardship.

Short sale is a time-consuming process, and you need to start out with a pretty clear expectation of success and a nice profit for your efforts.

### *Lender Contact & Documents*

First, get the homeowner's permission in writing to negotiate on their behalf with the lender. They may take your document, but check with the lender for their document package if they have one. Banks love forms and rules, so starting out with what they want to see is going to move things along a little faster.

Sit down with the homeowner to go through their financial situation, and it quickly gets personal. You'll be helping them convince the bank that a discounted short sale is preferable to a foreclosure, so you'll need to know everything about their financial situation.

- Every debt: mortgages, second mortgages, credit cards, store accounts, medical bills, car loans, etc.
- Any changes in their salary or employment situation that make it more difficult for them to make their payments.
- Medical situations that will be costly moving forward, such as a cancer diagnosis with future treatment and/or surgery.

It's not going to be comfortable for them or you, but it is absolutely necessary for the hardship letter.

### *The Hardship Letter & Documentation*

This letter is written to the bank to explain the financial situation of the borrower and why they are no longer able to afford their mortgage payments. It's not to get sympathy, as there isn't any of that at the bank. It's to convince the lender that the situation is terrible and it looks like foreclosure and/or bankruptcy is in the works.

Whether typed or handwritten, this needs to be in the words of the homeowner. It shouldn't sound like an investor pitch or a legal document. Supporting documents, such as mortgages, notes, loan statements, medical statements, and credit card statements will be included to prove the statements in the hardship letter.

Help the homeowner to gather every document that will prove financial hardship and verify the amounts owed and payments. Any letters from employers indicating pay cuts or possible layoffs should be in the document package. Since divorce is also a major reason for mortgage problems, a copy of the divorce decree and settlement should be included as well. Even if this is a solid marriage, if a previous divorce is costing money in alimony or child support, the documents that prove the amounts need to be included.

Credit reports should also be in the package. If the homeowner has kept previous printed copies of credit reports that show their score is dropping, put them into the packet and point this out. You're proving increased risk to this lender.

Tax returns are necessary as well, as they help to validate the other documents. The banks know that the tax return is most likely accurate, as the penalties for false return information are rough. If the tax return shows declining income, especially for the self-employed, this helps in proving hardship.

### *The Offer and Contract*

You'll be presenting an actual offer to buy at the price you hope will be accepted. The contract form you use should be commonly used in your state, or it should be one blessed by your attorney. If you can get a copy of a contract used statewide by real estate agents, it will be one the bank recognizes and works with all of the time.

This is like any other purchase offer we discuss in the book, in that you and the seller (the bank, not the homeowner) are going to negotiate a deal. The homeowner is not the seller, and they normally aren't allowed to receive any funds from the deal. It's a lot like negotiating with a lender on a bank-owned foreclosure property.

It's like a foreclosure negotiation in some ways, but now the bank has a choice to make. They'll be running a lot of numbers to cover the back of whoever has to sign and accept your final offer. This brings us to the other really important document submitted.

### *Your Property Market Valuation*

Just like beauty, value is in the eye of the beholder, but you're going to have to convince this lender that the current market value of the home if it goes to foreclosure is not going to be a better result than taking your short sale offer. You don't have to deal with their costs of foreclosure, as they know those numbers. However, one resource puts the average cost of a foreclosure to the bank nationally at around $50,000. This varies depending on whether it's a judicial or non-judicial state.

Your job is to submit a CMA type of valuation, but with a very different goal than the real estate agent's CMA for a seller. While a real estate agent will avoid using foreclosures as comps, you want to use them. They're selling well below market value of an owner occupied home in the retail market.

Use the CMA process, but gather comps from foreclosure sales in the area. Do a thorough job, and create a strong case for the offer price you're submitting. You want to use every negative factor you can find. Note in a supplement any condition problems, repairs necessary, etc. Take photos (or get them off the Web) of similar foreclosure properties selling at or below your offer and similar to this home. Definitely look for comps of properties that look better, are larger, or have better features, but sold for less than your offer in foreclosure.

You're convincing the bank that they're not going to do better going forward to foreclosure or bankruptcy. In fact, you want to convince them that they'll do much worse. Make this a thorough and professional CMA, and make sure that every comp is real and the numbers are accurate. They will definitely check.

### *Submit and Wait – Follow Up*

Once you submit the short-offer package, don't sit back and relax. When you submit, ask what their normal timeline is for a first response and a normal short sale process to closing. Then hold them to that with update requests if you're not hearing anything. You don't want to give them deadlines, but you do want to make them understand that your offer isn't going to be valid forever.

## Perspectives & Progress

You may not want to consider short sales now. But if you have any plans to do rental property investing or to sell to rental investors, you may want to explore how it is working in your area. This is especially true if you don't want to do fix & flips, as you can choose short sale opportunities based on the homes being in ready-to-rent condition.

Begin to gather short sale sold prices and home information for your files by neighborhood. Having this information ready for reference gives you a jump on the process, which can make the difference with a foreclosure sale looming in the near future.

---

### Chapter 15

## *Bird Dogging*
## *The Cash Challenged Business*

*"Who gets the bird, the hunter or the dog?" – John Lewis*

When you bird dog for another investor, your job is to locate potential investment deals for them. The quote above is a good question. The investor is the hunter, and they definitely get the bird. But you're going to get a treat, a fee, or a commission for pointing out the bird.

If you Google "real estate bird dog," you'll get thousands of results. Some will be pitching the concept, maybe selling a course or something. Others will say that it's not a valid concept, that you can't make money as a bird dog. Many people try it and don't make money, but it's like any other business. There is a right way to do it and several wrong ways.

Bird dogging for other investors is a great way to get started if you're cash poor. You don't need to buy any equipment, take on any overhead, or put up any money. If you work outdoors and move around, you can even do a lot of the legwork in the course of your regular daily activities.

How much money can you make? Like any other business, and like strategies in this book, it depends on the value that you deliver. That value is in the quality of the potential investment deals you bring to your buyer customer. You're constantly building that buyer list full of active investors. Real estate investment clubs are a great place to meet investors and ask if you can bring them deals. Your value, what you deliver, should be targeted on what they want and what they view as a profitable opportunity:

- **A wholesaler** – The wholesaler generally does little or nothing to improve or change the property. They simply locate opportunities for investment, lock them up through an assignment or purchase contract, and then flip them to another investor. The value you deliver is in locating deals they aren't finding on their own.
- **The fix & flip investor** – You're still locating deals they haven't found, but they should be homes that are going to yield a nice profit from a rehab and resale to a rental property investor or retail customer. You're looking for homes that need work.
- **The rental home investor** – Now you generally don't want homes in need of anything more than cosmetic repairs. The rental investor wants a home that they can quickly fill with a tenant for a positive cash flow. They'll also want it to be one they can buy at a discount to value.

How much you're paid will depend on their perception of the value you deliver as well as the actual profit your customer will make. If you're just driving around locating apparently abandoned homes and providing an address to an investor, you may see only $50 +/- per lead. If you give them more productive than non-productive leads, you could keep a small income stream going.

If you're willing to wait for a successful closing, then just delivering an address could result in a higher payout, maybe hundreds of dollars. There's less risk to the investor because they're not spending any money for leads that don't get to a closing. The key to bird dog income is handing an investor a profit gift.

## What You're Doing

Basically, at this level, you're simply keeping your eyes open and scouting around for homes that could be a great investment for certain investor buyer types. You know what each investor needs for a profitable deal, and you let them know the address of homes you think may work for them.

You don't need any cash to do this other than for gas to drive around and scope out opportunities. You may see a home with tall grass in the yard, newspapers in the driveway, and no furniture in the house. It could be that the owners moved out when they couldn't make their payments and they needed to move for a new job. It's a possible future foreclosure, and by catching it early you could be giving an investor the opportunity to contact the owners and buy it.

There are other clues besides the grass and newspapers. An empty hole where the electric meter goes is a sure sign there is no one living in the home. A tag on the gas meter with it locked off is another. A quick questioning of the neighbors can get you the information you need.

Another way you can turn up potential deals is to put the information out there about what you're doing. Telling your family and friends that you are a pipeline connecting distressed sellers with cash buyers can get leads handed to you. Nobody else knows about them, and you simply pass them along.

Yet another productive deal-finding strategy is to get to know people whose jobs get them early notice of homes no longer occupied. From electric meter readers/techs, to mail persons or gas company or newspaper employees, they're all good resources. If you can get these people to let you know about homes that are going vacant, it's an early warning system for profits.

## Higher Level Bird Dogging for Higher Payouts

The image at the top of this chapter symbolizes a more lucrative bird dogging strategy. Now, instead of handing them just a possible deal, you're wrapping it up in a pretty package. That package is your understanding of their requirements and your due diligence so they have less to do and a much higher conversion of leads to closings.

I like the idea of calling this group "deal drones" because they're like flying drones that have sophisticated sensors, cameras, and other equipment to gather information. They're not simply pointing out a possible good deal. They're evaluating the potential and presenting it with data to prove it's a great deal for a specific type of investor. It's almost like the bird dog taking the shot for the hunter. There are people out there making $2,500 to $5,000 or more on every deal with some really major investors.

The added value that makes you worth this kind of money is your complete understanding of exactly the type of deal the investor wants. You know how they evaluate a home, calculate market value, and decide what they're willing to spend.

- **Wholesaler** – You know the type of investors they have on their buyer list. You know the price range they work in and what they want for a profit, so you can prep the deal to know approximately what they'll have to pay for the home, and it will be low enough for their desired profit. In other words, you do most of what they were going to do, and you wrap it up into a ready-to-do deal package with the data to back it up.

- **Fix & Flip** – You need a lot more knowledge to be of real value to this investor. You need the wholesaler stuff above, plus the knowledge to come up with at least a close ballpark of what they'll pay for a home and what they'll spend to get it ready for sale to their customer. When you bring them the deal, you bring an ARV, After Repair Value, calculation, as well as a spreadsheet of estimated rehab costs and an estimate of what they'll have to pay for the home.

- **Rental home investor** – Now you're dealing with a buyer who wants a home ready for a renter, and it needs to be bought at a discount to current market value. They want to lock in equity from day one. They also want a home that will rent with a nice positive cash flow. Your ability to "run the numbers," considering current market rents as well as costs to own and maintain the home, will be your added value.

To get the higher bird dog (bird drone) payouts, you need to become a kind of alter-ego of your buyer customer. You think like they think, and evaluate the deal exactly like they would. This allows you to deliver a ready-to-go deal that they recognize immediately as one they would love to have found on their own. You can have a fee arrangement agreed upon in advance, and many just have a set amount for every deal that goes to closing.

## When Contracts aren't Desired

There are investors who do these higher level bird dog deals as their only business. They don't want to tie up their money or take any risk in contract negotiations and transfer of ownership. It's simple, becomes a well-learned strategy, and the investor sticks with what works. However, many take the next and much more profitable step to wholesaling.

---

## Perspectives & Progress

Bird dogging may be the place you want to start, as you may be pretty overloaded with work and family obligations and light on cash. You're out and about every day, so begin to pay attention to the homes you pass. Build relationships with people who can give you advance notice of vacant homes. Even if you don't bird dog, these homes are profit opportunities for every other strategy in this book.

Continue to learn the strategies in the book so you can either do them yourself or apply your knowledge to a higher level of bird drone activity to get higher commissions for your leads.

### Chapter 16

# *Wholesaling:*
# *Profitable in any Marketplace or Time*

*"It's about listening first, then selling" – Erik Qualman*

You know what's great about this photo of a wholesale truck being unloaded? It shows us the tip of the iceberg in terms of what we won't be paying for in our successful real estate wholesaling business! We're going to be a profitable wholesaler without:

- Trucks.
- Fuel and maintenance of a truck fleet.
- Employees to drive the trucks.
- Employees to stock the warehouse.
- Massive piles of cash to buy from manufacturers in bulk.
- Warehouses.
- Insurance on offices, warehouses, and inventory.
- Liability and vehicle insurance.

There's more, but you get the idea. A traditional wholesaler of goods has a huge overhead burden to produce a small markup between the manufacturer/distributor and the retailer. It takes deep pockets to get started and a heavy volume to maintain profit margins.

Though we can if we want, we don't need to buy our inventory before we sell it. We don't have to store it, insure it, or transport it. We don't need employees to manage the business, and we don't need an office. The kitchen table will do. So what do we need?

- The skills we discussed in the bird dog chapter that help us find homes for our investor buyers.
- The ability to market for distressed sellers and to negotiate to buy their homes at discounts that will allow us a profit and still be a good deal for our buyers. But we don't have to actually buy, as you'll see.
- A good buyer list with investors who welcome our deals and will pay cash.

We see three items related to abilities and a list of buyers, but nothing there about money. That's because there is no need for a lot of cash to be a real estate wholesaler. The most you're going to commit to a deal is an earnest money deposit, and it's going to come back to you by closing. This can be as little as under $100 to a few hundred dollars in most cases. Skip Starbucks for a few months to take care of this.

## Listen, and then Sell

As the quote says at the beginning of the chapter, you listen first, then sell. You listen to what your investor buyers want, make sure you record and understand that information thoroughly, and then deliver exactly what they want. It's like that bird drone strategy of becoming their alter ego. However, unlike the bird drone, you're going to become a party to the transaction(s).

You're not going to be successful at wholesaling unless you do a really good job of keeping a file of what your buyers want and how they evaluate a property to decide if it's a good deal for their investment portfolio or strategy. The difference in wholesaling is that you're taking an ownership or control position in the subject property. You become a middle person in the deals. This doesn't need to mean ownership or liability. Let's take a look at the two ways in which to wholesale real estate.

## The Any Market Strategy

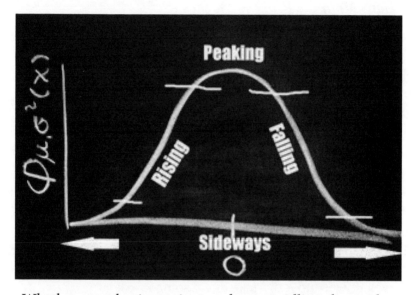

Whether a market is moving up, down, or idling along sideways, wholesaling is an investment strategy that you can use for profits. Even in the worst of times, people are buying, selling, and renting homes. Sure, they may be buying fewer of them, but if that is the case, then rental demand is rising.

### The Rising Market Wholesaler

When things are rocking along, as they were for a couple of decades leading up to around 2000, there was a healthy demand for homes. There was plenty of new construction, but rising home values were just as positive for existing homes. People were upsizing, buying up in value, and in general enjoying a good housing economy. If you were wholesaling then, you would probably have been locating existing homes that needed upgrading to more modern floor plans and features.

Because home prices were rising steadily, there were remodel investors able to rehab these homes and make a tidy profit. It was a little more of a challenge to locate the deals because there weren't as many motivated and distressed sellers, but they were out there. The wholesaler's value added was in finding those deals.

### Caution in the Peaking Market

The almost irrational boom that started building up through most of 2006 was different. The market was crazy, with homes selling at a profit after only weeks of ownership. Fix & Flip was working great, but just flipping them with no improvements was making a lot of money quickly for many flippers and wholesalers. This was a peaking market, however, and prices were ready to correct in late 2006 and early 2007, depending on location.

The beginning of the downturn was much more than just a correction; it was a full-blown crash. There are plenty of fingers pointing in many directions to place the blame, but it really doesn't matter to the investor unless you were holding some inventory when the sudden run downward began. This is one situation where over-extending yourself to take advantage of crazy profits could take you down; and it did take down some investors.

The key to survival when things seem to be rocking along as if there is no end to good times is to know that there will be an end at some point. Don't overextend your financing or take on too many deals just because you don't want to miss some profit opportunities.

In this risky "times are great" market, the wholesaler is really at an advantage. Because the wholesaling concept is one with short-term holding periods (usually 30 – 45 days), your risks are lower. The fix & flip investor carries greater risk, as the holding and rehab period can be months.

### The Falling Market

Though the period after 2006 was more of a free falling market, there were real estate investors making money. From 2007 through 2011, there were around four million foreclosures. Some of the finger-pointing was on target in blaming lenders for making risky loans to people who couldn't afford them. Many of those people lost their homes during this period.

But, these homeowners were for the most part still employed and needing shelter for themselves, so they became renters. After enjoying their own home, they wanted to rent a single family home more than an apartment, so rental demand grew steadily. Investor buyers with cash were scooping up foreclosure homes in massive numbers and converting them to rental properties.

The wholesaler did really well during this period because their added value came from sifting through many properties to deliver the jewels to the rental investors. Locating a deep discount foreclosure in ready-to-rent condition brought wholesalers high profits on quick turnover deals.

### *Sideways Markets*

Though there's been a lot of media attention placed on pockets of rising home prices from 2011 forward, they're not indicating an overall rising market. Buyer demand is still historically very low. First time homebuyers are almost nonexistent. Historically that group has made up a big part of improving markets. The economy and jobs issues are keeping many members of the millennial generation living at home with their parents.

Overall, it's been more of a sideways market, with a lot of uncertainty in the near term. People are still recovering from credit rating woes after foreclosure, and they're not able to take advantage of historically low interest rates. Without consistent and growing buyer pressure, sideways may be the market condition for a while.

The wholesaler is smiling all the way to the bank, though. Foreclosure inventories are down, but rental demand and rents have been climbing fast. The rental investor is struggling to find deals that were falling into their laps a few years ago. The wholesaler uses their marketing and other property location skills to turn up opportunities. Then they run the numbers to match a seller's deal with a buyer on their list. Profits follow.

Even fix & flip buyers are clamoring for deals because the rental home buyers are asking them for upgraded properties to meet the desires of today's renters. If the numbers work, the wholesaler can find one or more buyers for every property they can dig up.

We've just moved through every market cycle, and we see that there is a way for a wholesaler to profit all the way through. Sure, your strategies will need to adapt to the market, but the great news is that there is a strategy for up, down, or sideways market movement. Now let's see how the process of wholesaling works; how we become a part of the transaction for higher profits.

## The Assignment Contract

You've been running ads, placing bandit signs, and searching high and low for motivated sellers. You've found one, and the numbers look good. The home is owner-occupied, and they have equity, but really need to sell to relocate for employment reasons. The home is ready to rent, so you check your buyer list for rental property investors who want homes in this area of town.

You've worked hard to build up a strong buyer list, and there are at least two or three investors you know who will have an interest in this property. Just in case, you call them to make sure they're still in the game, and all three are still looking for deals. You've been keeping files of sold properties in the area, and you do a CMA on the home. Even giving your rental investor a 10% discount to current market value, you know you can buy this home at a price and make around $5,500 on a wholesale deal.

You negotiate with the owner until you reach a number that works for you. The deal is set, and a purchase contract is the next step. You'll be doing this as an assignment deal. Here's the major way the assignment deal differs on the contract, and it's only a few words. Here's the normal way the contract starts out:

*Buyer: _____YOU_____ agrees to purchase from Seller: _____ for the price.....*

In an assignment deal, we just add a few words to the buyer line.

*Buyer: _____YOU, and or assigns (or assignees)_____*
*agrees to purchase from Seller.......*

You'll want to use a contract your attorney approves, and there will be some additional language, but this is the major difference between a regular purchase contract and an assignment contract. Check legality and requirements in your state.

What have you agreed to do and what are you obligated to do in this deal?

- You have agreed to buy the home for a specified price and according to all other terms of the contract.
- However, you have also had the seller agree that you have the right to assign your rights and obligations to someone else. That would be your ultimate buyer.
- When you do an assignment contract with your buyer, you no longer have anything to do with this deal. You're no longer obligated to buy the home, nor do you have any rights in the transaction.
- You are at risk for the earnest money deposit.

Let's talk about earnest money. It can be hundreds of dollars, thousands of dollars, or in some cases under $100 if you have a highly motivated seller. This is a part of the negotiation. If you are unable to assign the deal, do you have to buy the property? Many contracts can be enforced when the buyer is in default through a "specific performance" lawsuit. The seller can sue to force the buyer to go through with the deal. Judges can only really issue a judgment against you for the purchase price, not force you to buy.

This is where you can avoid a problem with the right language in the contract. It should state that the seller's sole remedy for the buyer's default is the forfeiture of the buyer's earnest money deposit. This limits your risk to that amount in almost every case.

### Assigning the Deal

You now control this property for the period of the contract. If you set a closing date 30 to 45 days out, you need to get cracking on assigning the deal. Your buyer will want as much time as possible for their closing transaction tasks and due diligence. You already know which buyers you'll be pitching, so it's a quick process. You'll be out of the deal immediately upon assignment.

The assignment contract is relatively short, but important, so get it written or approved by your attorney. It has one purpose: to assign all of your rights AND obligations over to your buyer at the price you negotiate. Once you do that, you're off the hook, and only waiting for your payday at closing.

What about the earnest money? Especially after you've worked with an investor for a while, you may be able to negotiate some or all of your profit to be paid at the time of assignment. It may be just the amount of the earnest money, or some other amount. It's more likely, however, that you'll get most or all of your compensation paid at the closing table.

The title company or attorney handling the closing will get copies of both your purchase contract with the seller and your assignment contract. The settlement statement will take care of payment for the property, your payment, and closing costs, which are now the responsibility of the other two parties,.

Using assignment contracts is a great way to control the deal, increase your profits, and minimize your risk in a wholesale deal. You bring a clean deal to your buyer which is already negotiated on the seller end, and you are ready to move to closing. You can spend an entire real estate investment career just doing assignment deals with minimal cash invested.

### *Regular Purchase Contract and Flip to Investor Buyer*

In the assignment deal, the buyer knows your purchase price because they're taking over that contract. This can lead to lower profits, since they're negotiating with that knowledge. If you straight-out purchase the other property and immediately resell it to your buyer, they're not a party to your purchase.

This type of deal has been called a "back-to-back" closing or a "double closing." Before the real estate crash and subsequent stricter regulations, you could get the title companies to fund the first deal with the proceeds of the second, as the closings sometimes happened only minutes apart. Few companies will do this anymore. They want the purchase closing fully funded before you sell the property to your buyer.

These days it's still possible to do this type of deal with your only out-of-pocket expense being your earnest money, but it just adds an extra funding step. We'll get into funding resources in the next chapter. You can do this type of deal with the purchase closing followed closely by the sale to your buyer.

There is more profit to be made using this strategy. You know what your buyer is willing to pay, usually before you finalize the deal on the purchase. You know the market, have done your CMA to know the property value, and you also know that your buyer will purchase at a specified discount to market value. The better the deal you negotiate with the seller, the higher your profits, possibly even in the five figures for successful wholesalers.

---

### Perspectives & Progress

Begin to look into the types of purchase and assignment contracts used in your area. Get some advice from an attorney if necessary to be certain that you will be using the right legal documents for your deals. Wholesaling is such a great strategy, you'll want to get your ducks in a row.

Even if your interest is solely in rental property investment, you're going to be out there evaluating deals, and some aren't going to work for your rental property strategy. But they may work very well for wholesaling to another investor. An example would be a home needing more work than you're willing to invest, but the price is right. You can wholesale it to a fix & flip investor.

### Chapter 17

## *Funding Your Deals: The Money is Out There*

*"I would borrow money all day long, if the cost of borrowing is less than the expected return." – Brad Schneider*

The quote says it all for investors. If you can leverage the money you borrow for a significantly higher return than the cost of the loan, then it's probably a good decision. As the image suggests, few of us have tons of cash, so borrowing can fuel the growth of our business.

This chapter is very important if you are cash challenged, as you're going to see that there is a load of money out there if you just know where to go and how to approach the cash-holder. You shouldn't rule out any of the investment strategies you'll learn simply because you think you can't fund them.

Too many investors overlook funds they have available without going to commercial lenders. However, if you have a great wholesale deal opportunity, there are specialty resources just for your business. We're going to talk later about mortgages for rental properties. This chapter is about short-term financing for other strategies. Let's take a look at a number of ways to fund your deals.

## Tapping Home Equity

Many of us have a home and we've built up equity over the years by paying down our mortgage. There's a very flexible source of funds available through a HELOC, Home Equity Line of Credit. The bank or lender determines how much equity you have in your home and pre-approves a line of credit amount.

This is super flexible because you aren't getting a check. The line of credit sits there waiting for you to access it. You can write a check against it when you need it. Wholesaling is a great strategy for this type of loan, as you're going to pay it back in full quickly, cutting your interest costs. Some deals make thousands of dollars with just a few hundred paid in interest costs.

## Credit Cards

If you have credit cards with large unused balances, they can be a short-term resource for your deals. The interest rate is higher, but you're normally only going to pay interest through one or maybe two billing cycles, depending on timing. Don't forget to factor this into your deal costs when calculating your profit goal. If you happen to have a new card that allows checks and is offering free interest for six months or a year, you have a free financing resource for wholesale deals.

## Borrowing Against Retirement Accounts

This is one resource that is often overlooked. In many cases, you can borrow against a 401k or IRA for investment purposes. You'll normally have a specified period of time to replace the money, and you'll want to do that, since there will be penalties if you miss the deadline. Check with your retirement account administrator to see if you can access funds.

## Self-directed Retirement Accounts

This is a bigger step, but could be well worth it if you have significant money sitting in a 401k or IRA, and you're not happy with your returns. In this setup, you'll be able to actually invest in real estate in the account, but the rules are strict and complicated, and you don't want to run afoul of them, as it can be a tax nightmare.

Most people's retirement account custodians are not going to allow real estate investment. They stick to stocks, bonds, and traditional investments. You'll need to transfer your account to a custodial firm that allows self-directed investments. It's even better to search for a firm that's financially strong and experienced in real estate investment.

That's because every transaction, every expense, and every rent check or income item, MUST be handled not by you personally, but through the account. Messing this up will cost you a bundle in taxes. The good news is that your investment portfolio is growing with deferred taxes due to the retirement account benefits. You won't be able to deduct expenses, however, as there is no taxable income.

**Self-Directed Accounts - AccuPlan.net**
www.accuplan.net/Retirement_Accounts ▾ (800) 454-2649
Proactively Manage Your Retirement Account With A Self-Directed IRA!
Invest In Real Estate                 Precious Metals Investing
Self-Directed 401Ks                   IRA Checkbook Control

**Self directed real estate IRA - iDirectLaw.com**
www.idirectlaw.com/ ▾
Place IRA/401k Funds Into Alternate Investments Like Real Estate & More

**PENSCO Self Directed IRA - Pensco.com**
www.pensco.com/ ▾ (888) 481-3509
Invest in Real Estate, Notes, Private Equity with Tax Advantages!
Fraud Prevention - Contact Us - About Us - Learn

**How to Use a Self-Directed IRA to Buy Real Estate | Fox ...**
www.foxbusiness.com/.../how-to-use-self-directed-... ▾ Fox Business Network ▾
May 8, 2012 - Here are five things to keep in mind when considering investing in real estate through a self-directed IRA.

**Using a Self Directed IRA LLC To Purchase Real Estate**
www.irafinancialgroup.com/llcpurchaserealestate.php ▾
Few Investors realize that the IRS has always permitted real estate to be held inside IRA retirement accounts. Investments in real estate with a Self-Directed IRA ...

**Real Estate IRA Center | The Entrust Group**
www.theentrustgroup.com/investments/real-estate-ira/ ▾ The Entrust Group ▾
The Self-Directed Real Estate IRA Center was created for those who are interested in learning about investing in real estate with a self-directed ira

**self directed retirement account**
www.broadfinancial.com/Retirement_Acct ▾
Self Direction + Checkbook Control.
Best IRA for Real Estate Investing!

**Fidelity IRA**
www.fidelity.com/ ▾
A Fidelity IRA has the Options You
May Need. Get Started Today.

**Self Directed Solo 401(k)**
www.irafinancialgroup.com/ ▾
(800) 472-0646
Invest in Real Estate+More Tax Free
No Custodian Fee- Free Consultation

**USAA Retirement Guide**
www.usaa.com/Retirement ▾
Guidance for every stage of
retirement planning. View today.

**Retirement Properties**
www.homeunion.com/retirement-property ▾
Get Monthly Rental Cash-flow.
Sign-up Now for Further Information

**T. Rowe Price IRA**
www.troweprice.com/ ▾
Open An IRA Account. Benefit From
Proven Performance & Low Cost.

The screenshot of a Google search on *"self-directed retirement account for real estate"* shows that there are plenty of firms out there offering this type of account for real estate investors. This is your future, so do a very thorough investigation to make sure you're choosing a financially stable and experienced custodian.

## Partnerships

Once you become active in real estate investment and perhaps joined a local real estate investment club, partnerships could be a financing resource. There will be other investors with cash challenges, and sometimes pooling your resources in a few deals can get you into shape to continue solo.

Consult an attorney to get the arrangement on paper with clear terms for responsibilities and splits. Sometimes you can even partner with your buyer, though this will reduce your profits. They're not in the banking business, and they'll want a return on their investment. However, if you consistently deliver great deals, they'll be easier to deal with.

## Family and Friends

If Uncle Henry is sitting on fat savings accounts and certificates of deposit and complaining about the tiny interest rates he's earning, you're looking at a resource. All of the quotes about not borrowing from relatives still apply, but you're in a different situation. They could be coming to you, instead of you going to them and asking for help.

Once you've done some deals and have a track record of success, your friends and family will take notice. You're consistently pulling double-digit returns on your deals while they're getting around 1% to 3% on their savings accounts. Inflation is nullifying those tiny rates. They will see that you know what you're doing and may want to invest in your success.

Investors are not only tapping this resource for wholesaling, they're also partnering with relatives in buying rental homes. Uncle Henry would love a consistent cash flow and an appreciating asset.

If you structure things properly with the help of a lawyer, you can become partners and set up reversion of ownership to you if your uncle dies. In some states this can be as simple as recording the deed as joint ownership with right of survivorship.

## The More Formal Solution

So far we've talked about resources you may already have but haven't tapped. They're also going to be the least expensive options. However, if you're unable or unwilling to use any of those solutions, there is an entire industry out there designed just for real estate investor short-term financing.

They're called transactional lenders, and they profit by loaning real estate investors short-term funds in return for fees and either interest or a flat percentage of the money loaned. It's not an inexpensive way to borrow, so you'll want to be sure of your costs to factor them into your deal.

Let's look at an example of a wholesale deal and how the funding works. You're going to be executing a normal purchase agreement with a motivated seller and selling the home to a buyer at a price that is $15,000 higher. It's not an assignment deal; you're signing to purchase.

You want to set up these transactions to close on the same day, or maybe one day apart, and you need financing to close the purchase and pay for that home until you can get the sale side closed. The transactional lender looks at your contracts but is not really concerned with your personal credit.

If they see good agreements and a buyer with proven cash resources, they will do the deal. As they do more deals with you, it gets faster and easier to get approvals, and you can have your deals pre-approved to lessen your risk in signing to buy that home. You're still really only at risk for the earnest money.

The transactional lender funds the purchase at closing and collects their repayment at the closing with your buyer. They get their loan repaid and profits at that closing, the buyer gets the home, and you get your profit minus the costs of the loan.

Here's an example chart from a transactional lending website:

| $1,000 minimum below $50,000 and 2% up to $250,000, 3% over that | $495 per deal | 48 Hour Minimum |
|---|---|---|

If you're grossing $15,000 on this deal and this is the only resource, it could be worth it. If you're borrowing $90,000, this rate schedule would result in around $2,295 in costs for you. You're still netting more than $12,000.

## Money isn't Your Problem

As you can see, there's lots of money out there, and many ways to get it to fund your deals. Money isn't the problem. Learning how to do deals, value properties, negotiate with sellers, and work with buyers is far more important.

---

### Perspectives & Progress

It's time to look at every funding resource in this chapter and see how they fit into your current situation. You just may find that you have what you need in personal resources to jump in with both feet. If not, you can begin to investigate transactional lenders to get a relationship started.

You want to be prepared with funding resources when you really begin to seriously pursue deals. It's not fun to find a really profitable deal that you're sure of, only to have to pass on it for lack of short-term funding.

---

### Chapter 18

# *Fix & Flip Basics:*
# *Project Structure and Profits*

*"It is a very sobering feeling to be up in space and realize that one's safety factor was determined by the lowest bidder on a government contract." – Alan Shepherd*

Alan Shepherd's quote about low bids and government contracts is both funny and a warning. In the right relationship with the right general contractor, you can do more deals because you can devote less time to job supervision. But, if you take a low bid with minimal specifications, it can be a disaster.

One reason the space shuttle seems to have few defects is because there are volumes of detailed engineering specifications on which the contractors bid. Then inspectors diligently check to make sure that those specifications are followed. You can't just drop your future and profits into the hands of a general contractor and walk away to buy another home.

In this chapter, we'll look at different ways to structure a rehab project, including supervision and responsibility. You have choices, and the tradeoff is your involvement in time and money. First, let's get an overview of fix & flip for the real estate investor.

## What is Fix & Flip?

The word "fix" is pretty self-explanatory, and this strategy is used on homes that need "fixing." They are in some stage of disrepair, from minor cosmetic work to major rehabilitation and remodel. The value added by the fix & flip investor over and above locating good deals, is in the fixing. Terrible looking homes are great candidates if their ARV, After Repair Value, will support the cost of the rehab plus a nice profit.

The worse they look, the less competition to buy them and the lower the purchase price. There's a lot of flexibility in negotiating the purchase and balancing that with rehab costs and the projected price the investor will get in a sale.

The players involved are mostly the same as in wholesaling:

- The investor doing the fix & flip.
- A motivated seller or a foreclosure property.
- An investor or retail buyer, more investors than retail.

The extra puzzle piece in fix & flip is the rehab of the home. The reason fix & flip is almost always a higher profit margin investment strategy than wholesaling and others is that there is much more value added. The fix phase is where the investor can build in more profits between the cost of the work and its value in the sale.

### When does it work?

The great news is that fix & flip works in every market cycle: rising, falling, and moving sideways. There will always be homes in poor repair, always some foreclosures in bad condition, and there is always profit in bringing these homes up to full market sale condition. When markets are hot and prices are rising, fix & flip can get a higher margin for the repair work due to high home prices. In slower markets, the investor just has to adjust purchase prices downward as well as their material choices to shoot for a more value-conscious customer.

### *Do I need a lot of cash?*

So far we've given you some great strategies that require little or no money. Fix & Flip really isn't that much different. You'll just need to secure short-term, higher-cost financing if you don't have your own resources as we talked about in the funding chapter.

Some of the same transactional lenders you'll find for wholesale will finance fix & flip for longer periods of time. Of course, you're going to pay for this funding, and it's not cheap. An example: you have a home you can wholesale to a fix & flip investor for a $7,500 gross profit with $2,200 deducted for transactional funding, netting $5,300. If you do the fix & flip, your gross profit may be $28,000, and your cost for funding could be $7,700. That's an extra $15,000 in your pocket from only 30 to 90 days more time for the rehab.

### *What about construction knowledge?*

You definitely DO NOT have to be a do-it-yourselfer for this investment strategy. If you can't drive a nail and are scared of electricity, it doesn't make any difference. Sure, the more you know, the better you'll be able to evaluate the work product of your contractors. But you'll learn, and being even more careful until you do learn should serve you well.

There are three ways to handle a rehab project:

- Using a general contractor to handle most or all of the sub-contracting and material purchasing decisions and supervision.
- Hiring a project manager who doesn't bid the job, instead working for a salary and maybe a bonus structure.
- Doing it all yourself.

Let's contrast these choices starting with the last.

## You're the Contractor and Supervisor

This is a full hands-on approach, and can be the most profitable way to get the job done. But you'll certainly do fewer deals, so you may find that your net at the end of the year is lower, and you worked a lot harder than necessary.

Most highly profitable fix & flip investors end up using one of the other two methods and possibly a mix of the two. In the next chapter we'll dig into the details, materials pricing, subcontractor hiring, and all of those pieces of the puzzle that make the difference between profits and just a so-so deal.

## General Contractor

The general contractor takes over the entire job, usually after being the successful bidder for turnkey work. You set out the project details (specifications), and the general contractor bids to complete the job using subcontractors they select, and they normally select all the materials too. This means they'll be making some kind of markup on materials, as well as marking up their subcontractor bids for work.

### *Advantages*

If you've done a good job of specifying what you want, this can work for you. It frees you up to go find more deals and leverage your experience and abilities. You have a hard number for the work, knowing what your profit should be on completion and sale. You spend less time on job visits and supervision. The general contractor coordinates the subcontractors, which is a critical part of the project. You can't have a drywall sub closing up a wall before the electrician has completed wiring.

Once you've developed a relationship with a general contractor over several jobs, you can modify your contracts in ways that work for both of you. Perhaps you select and purchase materials and the contractor just supervises the work. They lose their markup on materials which can increase your profit margin.

You may want to work out some type of bonus incentive for early completion, as it costs you money when jobs stretch out and run up your financing costs. The right partnership can free you up for other profitable activities.

### *Disadvantages*

This is usually a more expensive approach. You shouldn't just take the low bid, as you frequently get what you pay for. The general contractor is taking on more responsibility and risk, so they will factor in a cushion to protect their profit, which will in turn cut into your bottom line. You're definitely going to be paying more for materials, and they can be a big chunk of the overall project cost. You can make this a little better with a cost-plus contract where the contractor shows you the material invoices and then they get an agreed-upon percentage over cost.

Especially in early relationships, you may find that you're still spending a lot of time at the job site because you're finding problems or misunderstandings related to your different interpretations of the rehab specifications. It can get messy when the general contractor has already installed countertops that in your mind are not what you specified.

It's your business, and you should run it the way that works for you. You can adapt the contractual arrangement in any way you want. After you've completed these two chapters on fix & flip, you'll have the information you need to make some big-picture decisions.

### *Compensation*

Usually, this is a fixed bid job, and the dollar amount is known up front when the contract is signed. There may be damages clauses if the contractor doesn't perform on time, and/or bonus clauses for better performance. An experienced quality contractor should provide a bid that is going to be the way the job goes without surprises. This is good for you from a planning perspective, but it's the most costly approach to rehab projects.

## Project Manager

The project manager will be performing the job of a general contractor, but with a different compensation structure. They need the skills of a general contractor, and they may have been one in the past. The project manager may not like the hassle and risk of fixed bid contracts, preferring a structure that gets them paid without too much risk. You can create more of a partnership with a project manager, as their compensation can be structured in a number of ways.

### *Advantages*

This is usually a less expensive approach than using a general contractor because you're going to control the purchase of materials and their costs, with no markup to the manager. You're also going to take more of a role in selecting subcontractors that provide the quality you want at good prices. You're not relying on a general contractor to do this and mark up their work.

The project manager will still supervise and coordinate all work, pick up materials or have them shipped to the job, and work with local code enforcement and inspectors. You get more time to pursue other profitable deals.

### *Disadvantages*

You will spend more time with a project manager than with a general contractor, as you'll be making more decisions and communicating them to your manager.

If you've chosen your project manager carefully, and they are as capable as a general contractor, this is still an excellent approach. The drawback is in finding this individual who has all of the abilities but doesn't want to be a general contractor with their own business.

### *Compensation*

How you pay a project manager is very customizable. Of course, a salary with possible performance bonuses is common. A set amount for the whole project regardless of estimated time to completion is another approach. Yet another method used successfully by many investors is to make them a partner in the profitability of the job. You can pay them a percentage of the final profit of the job. Now they're thinking about ways to get the job done right at a lower cost.

Combine these compensation methods any way that works for you and makes your project manager an enthusiastic team player in your projects. When $40,000 in work is projected for a project and the project manager works hard to get quality on time for $35,000, you're happy to reward them. One hybrid way to work the compensation and bonus issue is to pay them a bonus percentage of every dollar under budgeted cost if the quality is there.

This might look like this:

- The budgeted rehab cost is $55,000.
- In addition to regular compensation, you split savings 50/50, 40/60, or some other split for all savings under $55,000.
- If the job cost comes in at $46,000, the split would apply to a $9,000 savings. If you're splitting 50/50, the manager should be working hard to see that extra $4,500 when the home sells.

OK, this chapter is the EASY part of fix & flip! In the next chapter, I'll show you how the "profit is in the details."

## Perspectives & Progress

Whether or not you have an interest now in fix & flip, start paying attention to remodel projects you see in your local travels. Stop and check them out. Talk to the job foreman or workers if they don't mind the interruption.

You're starting a file of contractors and subcontractors you may want to call on in the future. Get a business card. Take a picture of the contractor's job sign in the yard (send it to your Evernote Trades notebook). See if you can find the purchase price of the home before and after rehab to see the margins investors are getting.

*Chapter 19*

---

## *Fix & Flip*
## *The Profit is in the Details*

*A contractor dies and arrives in heaven to be met by Saint Peter who congratulates him on having lived to be 160 years old. The contractor says, "But I died at 40." Saint Peter tells him that can't be true because they added up his time sheets. – Just a Joke*

I like this image because it looks complex, with lots of stuff happening. That's what a fix & flip is: a complex job with a whole lot of stuff going on.

But this is far from a problem because this is where you add value to this investment strategy, and it's how you make your money. The joke just points out one of the things you have to watch in a rehab project: your labor costs.

### Taking the Middle Road

In the previous chapter, we looked at using a General Contractor versus a Project Manager, or even going it on your own. If you want to make the most of this investment niche, your profits are limited by working one project at a time through to completion before starting the next one. Since we've already discussed turning over most of the process to a general contractor, in this chapter we're going to go at the process with a combination of self-involvement and a project manager. This allows you to be involved as necessary to protect your interests and control your costs while freeing up your time to kick off other projects. Doing this, you'll be working with your project manager in selecting and supervising sub-contractors and in shopping and purchasing materials.

## Making the Numbers Work

Let's go through our fix & flip discussion with a real-world example property. We'll look at how we'll select this home, how we'll estimate the rehab cost, how we'll determine what we can sell it for once we're finished with rehab, , and what we have to buy it for to make it work. Then we'll go over the job and its costs.

### _Our Project Home_

We've located a foreclosure home with condition problems that make it impossible for a normal buyer to get financed, but it may be a great project for fix & flip to a couple of rental investors on our buyer list. Characteristics:

- 3 bedroom, 2.5 baths
- Attached 2 car garage
- Typical subdivision lot size in the middle of the block
- 1950 square feet
- Rehab necessary:
    ○ New roof, composite type
    ○ Replace kitchen cabinets
    ○ Replace tubs, vanities in all 3 bathrooms
    ○ Low flush toilets X 3
    ○ Replace 12 windows with low-energy style
    ○ New tile for main living area
    ○ New carpet for 3 bedrooms
    ○ New appliances in kitchen

- ◦ New HVAC system
- ◦ Significant plumbing and electrical repairs
- ◦ Paint walls and ceilings, replace baseboards
- ◦ Replace exterior doors & garage door
- ◦ Some landscaping

Overall the home isn't too bad, though it looks horrible. This is a great opportunity if the buy and sell numbers work.

## ARV – After Repair Value

This is something we've already discussed in Chapter 9, the valuation of a home in the retail marketplace the way the Realtors do it. For fix & flip we're not starting with a home ready for sale. In fact, the less ready for sale the home is, the more profit potential there is in the rehab. The uglier the problems, at least to a point, the less we should have to pay for the home and the more profit we can build into the rehab portion of the job.

The market value created from a CMA type of process is the ARV, After Repair Value, of the home. We may be selling to a retail buyer, but a big market for fix & flip properties is made up of rental property investors. They're not going to pay full value, so we should decide at the beginning if we're working toward a retail sale or a discount sale to an investor. It's not absolutely necessary to know this, though. If you work every deal as if you're selling to an investor at a discount, you can change your mind and go retail for more profit. It doesn't work nearly as well going the other direction.

Whether we do a CMA ourselves or rely on a trusted resource, the ARV value of every prospective investment home must be our first evaluation item. We can locate cheap foreclosures all day, but they're not deals until we can buy, rehab, and sell at a profit. We start at the tail end by determining the ultimate value of each home we're considering.

### Our ARV Result

We've gathered good comps and determined that this home is worth $197,000 in the retail market. There is also pretty good demand in this neighborhood for both purchases and rentals. We're going to place this home with one of our rental investors, and we have a couple of them who consistently buy at 10% below value or so. We'll work for 12% as a discount, making our sale number $173,360.

### Rehab/Repair Cost Estimation

This process will evolve as you build relationships and successfully complete jobs. You may be able to rely on a contractor's estimates at some point. You shouldn't have to call out a contractor to do bids every time you find a possible new investment, though. You should at least know how to come up with a ballpark estimate of rehab cost to narrow down your choices.

As you build on your experience and get some profitable jobs under your belt, you'll be able to short-circuit this process and come up with a ballpark estimate so you can decide if you want to move forward and involve contractors in getting harder numbers.

There is competition in this business, so you'll want to get good enough at this to speed the process to avoid delay and loss of opportunities to buy. You'll also begin to build on your past jobs experience to make estimates easier when you find similar problems or repairs you've dealt with in the past. "Oh yeah, we had this same roofing situation on that house at 1234 Jones Street."

You can get a lot of great information and even localized project remodel estimates online. Let's look at some sites where you can get a reasonable ballpark estimate.

### HomeRenovationEstimate.com

This site gives us forms for entry of the repairs and remodel items on our list. There are a couple of really important things to remember about online estimates like these:

- They're usually not regionalized, and there can be big differences in what you pay from area to area.
- They're mostly for homeowners, not investors, so you're seeing retail costs. You should be paying considerably less

if you're controlling material purchases and doing good contractor selection.

All we're trying to do at this stage is to get a ballpark for rehab to subtract from our selling price to our investor to see the most we can pay for the home. It's still too early to make purchase decisions.

We're not going to go through all of them, but here are a couple of screenshots to show you how it works:

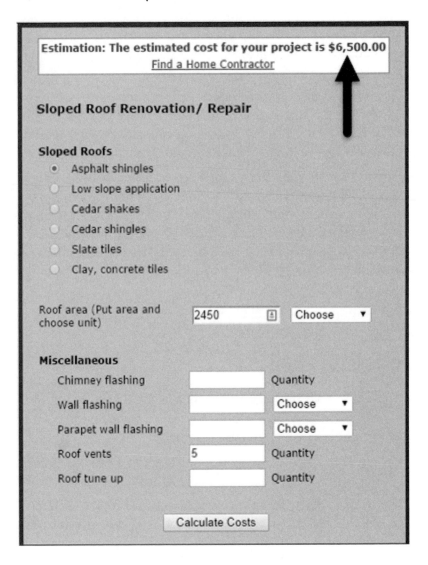

You can see our entries for roof area, type of roof, and number of roof vents/penetrations. The calculated cost is in the box at the top, showing $6,500.

**Estimate** Calculators

**Roof Renovation and Roof Repair**

Sloped Roofs — Estimate Costs

Flat Roofs — Estimate Costs

Exterior Wall Siding — Estimate Costs
alluminium, stucco & more..

Eavestroughs — Estimate Costs

Deck Construction — Estimate Costs

Patio Construction — Estimate Costs

Fence Construction — Estimate Costs

Driveways and Walkways — Estimate Costs

Landscaping — Estimate Costs

Garage Renovations — Estimate Costs

Windows : — Estimate Costs
Replacements and Window Installation

Exterior Doors — Estimate Costs
Installation and Build

Stairs and Railing Renovations

Bathroom : — Estimate Costs
Renovation and Bathroom Remodeling

Kitchen : — Estimate Costs
Renovation and Kitchen Remodeling

Floor Coverings — Estimate Costs

General Interiors — Estimate Costs

Fireplaces — Estimate Costs

From this screenshot of the menu calculation items, you can see that we can go through our project and estimate the items on our list one-by-one. We won't do this here, but you can see that we can get pretty detailed in our estimate.

We're working with retail, so we're definitely going to be higher than our actual costs. For now, let's just use the number this site comes up with for our next step in the process, because it has a built-in retail "fudge factor."

We ran through all of the items on our list, and the total comes to $29,474. Now we have a selling price and a cost to rehab to make the home ready to occupy.

$173,360 - $29,474 = $143,886

Part of our value in fix & flip is in the rehab. We could just work with the $29,474 number and take the difference between that and our actual cost to get the work done, or we could add more profit to that item. For now, let's just decide that the absolute most we can pay for this home is $143,886 minus the profit we want on the whole job.

The foreclosure is listed for sale at $124,500. If we paid that, we'd come out with $19,386 plus any profit on the rehab less closing costs. That's not enough for the time and risk involved, so we make a low offer and try to get the home for $107,500. In the interim we've also nailed down our material costs with our discount at a home improvement store, and we've gotten our sub-contractor bids.

We know that our rehab costs will actually be $23,900 instead of the retail estimate of $29,474. Now we have this for our profit calculation before closing (and funding) costs on both buy and sell sides:

$173,360 - $107,500 - $23,900 = $41,960

That's a pretty good result for maybe a month or so of our time. Deals this good and much better are happening every day. Once you know the selling price and a close estimate of rehab, you can negotiate hard to get the purchase price down and profits up. There are still some great foreclosure and distressed properties in almost every market that work for fix & flip. A regular retail buyer can't get normal financing to buy a home that isn't ready to occupy, so these are our stock in trade.

You can do a Google search for renovation estimation sites and find many of them. If you use one or more of these sites, keep in mind that it's just an estimate and that it is retail-oriented.

**Home Renovation Estimate:** Calculate Costs **Online**
www.homerenovationestimate.com/ ▾
WELCOME to Home Renovation Estimate. Calculate your Home Renovation Costs
Online. Our easy to use home renovation cost calculators allow you to get ...
Bathroom Remodeling ... - Kitchen Remodeling ... - Interior Renovations ... - Flooring

**Free Home Improvement** Resources, Calculators ...
www.improvenet.com/r ▾
Get a ballpark estimate of your pending project. Our exclusive estimators calculate the
cost of materials and installation keyed to your specific zip code. See how ...
You've visited this page 2 times. Last visit: 4/19/14

**Home Remodel Estimator** - Itemized costing guide for your ...
www.homeremodelestimator.com/ ▾
ITEMIZED, INSTANT, FREE ESTIMATES. Welcome to Home Remodel Estimator –
Unlike other estimating sites, we provide detailed, itemized, instant, and ...

**HomeAdvisor** - **Home** Repair Cost Guide
www.homeadvisor.com/cost/ ▾
Find real cost information from recently completed home projects in your city.
HomeAdvisor's Cost Guide allows you to find how much it will cost to complete your ...

**Real Remodeling** Costs - Houzz
www.houzz.com/remodeling-costs ▾ Houzz ▾
Avg. home value for those completing this project. $125K. Avg. household income for
those completing this project. --. Rank among the metros for % of people ...

Now that we know the process and money steps, let's get into some detail about how we contract the job and get those discounts on materials that can improve our profit picture. Instead of thinking of fix & flip as increasing risk because of the rehab piece, think of it as offering another profit center that wholesaling doesn't. We can get better at cutting our material and labor costs and increase our profits a lot.

## Materials Cost – Profit Opportunity

The obvious resource for construction materials is the big box home improvement store. A lot of the material used in our rehabs may come from *Lowe's, Home Depot,* or other similar stores. They all have some version of a contractor's desk, and they provide discounted prices to remodelers, contractors, and investors who set up accounts.

While you may use online project estimates for a big picture and narrowing down opportunities, when you get into a project, you want hard numbers. Develop a spreadsheet for materials used in a complete home remodel by room or area of the home. This spreadsheet is just about materials. You can probably get one from one of the contractors you know.

Your plan here is to walk through the home as the project manager or with your project manager, and enter the materials and quantities you need. Items like square yards of carpet, square feet of walls, appliances that must be replaced, windows, etc. are what you have on this sheet. Once you have the approximate quantities, you go to the home store and either you walk through and price each item, or you have the store's contractor desk do it for you, with any allowed discounts.

### Liquidators for Deep Discounts

Do a quick Google search for "building materials liquidator" and you'll probably find one or more of them in your area. They buy up odd lots, and they buy out contractors who have gone bankrupt or have completed projects with materials left over.

### Building Material Liquidation - Douglasville, GA ... - Facebook
https://www.facebook.com/.../Building-Material-Liquidation/197214136... ▾
Building Material Liquidation, Douglasville, GA. 587 likes · 1 talking about this · 17
were here. Local Business.

### Building supply liquidation buyers,closeouts buyers
www.aaacloseout.com/buildingsupply.html ▾
liquidators buyers,closeouts buyers,surplus buyers,overstock buyers,windows
buyers,doors buyers,building supply buyers.

### Surplus liquidation overstock closeout Deals!
www.coholiquidation.com/ ▾
Freight Liquidators specializing in OS&D , Distressed Freight, Overfreight and Shipping
Damage Sales. ... Building Materials. Industrial. Sporting Goods. Tools & ...

### LIQUIDATORS - Home
www.theliquidatorsatcumming.net/ ▾
The Liquidators at Cumming. We are a Building Material Surplus Supply Store in
Cumming Georgia. We offer Windows, Doors, Trim and More!

### Building Materials Outlet Midwest Inc. - The Handyman's ...
www.bmomn.com/ ▾
Building Materials Outlet is a family-owned business that has been successful in
liquidating and selling building materials for over 40 years. We now have three ...

### Commercial Liquidators
www.clofa.net/ ▾
Commercial Liquidators of America is one of Indianapolis, Indiana's largest liquidators

You can often buy materials from these liquidators for pennies
on the dollar. Every penny saved goes to the bottom line. If you're
working with a project manager, you can delegate the shopping
visits. Another resource you might not have considered is a local
*Habitat for Humanity ReStore.*

## Shop Habitat for Humanity ReStore

Whether you are a do-it-yourselfer, homeowner, renter, landlord, contractor, interior designer, environmentalist or treasure hunter, make Habitat for Humanity ReStore your first stop when shopping for your home or next renovation project.

The prices are great and you never know what you will find.

While most of what you find there will be used, they also sell new building materials and other items donated when they're left over at the end of projects.

## Working with Contractors and Subs

The ratio of labor to materials is different for every project, but the cost of labor is always a major component of fix & flip project cost. It's also a more complicated piece than materials. Remember the quote at the beginning of this chapter. A kitchen sink is a kitchen sink, but a labor time sheet can be a work of fiction.

Generally you'll be working with sub-contractors who will be paying their crew, and they'll have the responsibility to make sure they're showing up and getting paid for real work. However, you'll be the one responsible for paying subs, and you can't let them get ahead of your money. Get ahead of your money? That's getting paid for work not yet completed. You always want to be paying for work that is finished and checked for quality. A few other very important contractor-related considerations include:

- Checking their references.
- Checking their licensing and bonding.

- If possible, checking on any complaints filed against them with licensing authorities.
- Inspecting some of their past work.
- Having a written contract specifying when work will be started and completed, as well as specifying when payment will be made AFTER inspection of the work.
- If they're providing materials and need some advance payment to get them to the job, controlling the money carefully and making sure that the materials arrive as paid for.

Pay when you're supposed to and keep the good subs happy, as they're a big part of your profit and success. You'll get better bids for work and faster responses if you keep a smaller trusted group busy than you will trying to maintain a large group on standby.

## The Retail Margin Business

The majority of fix & flip investment is intended for purchase by rental property investors. However, there are retail buyers out there, and if you work it right, you can keep that discount in your pocket that you would have given to the investor buyer.

Better preparation and somewhat different criteria for property selection play into the retail market. While one area may be good for rentals, it may not be the best area to attract eager retail buyers. You're still doing all of the valuation stuff, job costing, and rehab work, but you're now considering upgrading materials for a different purchaser. You may upgrade items like flooring, countertops, appliances, and cabinets. Of course, you're still expecting a profit on these items and work, and you may even be able to sell the home for slightly over your value estimate.

If you move into higher price ranges, buyers of higher-end properties will often pay more for favored features and certain neighborhoods. You will need to change your cost outlook to include marketing expense and commissions, however.

---

## Perspectives & Progress

At this point in the book I've covered the most popular and profitable short-term real estate investment strategies, from bird dogging through wholesaling and fix & flip. You have enough knowledge to begin using these strategies for profits. Go back over them and decide where your comfort level is and start there.

If you have more long-term objectives, we're going to see how tens of thousands of investors have created comfortable and even lavish retirement lifestyles through rental property investment. One or more investment strategies in this book can work for you now. You just need to get started.

### Chapter 20

# Rental Property Investment: Building Long-Term Wealth

*"If you're not going to put money in real estate, where else?*
*– Tamir Sapir*

In October 2013, the National Multifamily Housing Council reported that 35% of households in the U.S. were occupied by renters. That's a lot of households, and the ratio of renters seems to be increasing. The housing market crash devastated the economy and created millions of new renters through foreclosure. Younger Americans watched this happening, so they are less inclined to jump into buying a home. First time homebuyer activity is still very low.

If you want to get a feel for the general outlook for the next few years in housing, do a Google search on "nation of renters."

**US risks becoming a nation of renters: Bank CEO - Yahoo ...**
finance.yahoo.com/.../u-risks-becoming-nation-renters-1...  ▾  Yahoo! Finance ▾
May 22, 2014 - From Yahoo Finance: There's a risk of the U.S. becoming a nation of
renters because of constraints on lenders, former Wells Fargo chairman ...

**A Nation of Renters: Should We Be Worried That Fewer ...**
business.time.com/.../a-nation-of-renters-should-we-be-worried-that...  ▾  Time ▾
Apr 26, 2013 - Big Wall Street banks and consumer-advocacy groups like the Center for
Responsible Lending don't agree on much. But recently, these ...

**Nation of Renters: Fewer Americans Now Own Their Own ...**
www.nbcnews.com/.../nation-renters-fewer-americans-no...  ▾  NBCNews.com ▾
Jul 29, 2014 - Home ownership in the United States has hit a 19-year low as tight
finances continue to drive Americans toward renting, one of the lasting ...

**Housing Starts: Is America Becoming a Nation of Renters?**
wallstcheatsheet.com/.../housing-starts-is-america-becoming-a-nation-of-...  ▾
May 16, 2014 - After a slow start to the year, housing starts in the United States surged
higher last month to easily beat expectations and dampen fears about ...

**Are We About To Become A Nation Of Renters? | Bankrate ...**
www.bankrate.com/finance/real.../nation-of-renters.aspx  ▾  Bankrate Inc ▾
Apr 24, 2013 - The percentage of U.S. households that owns a home has dropped
significantly in recent years, and experts say this downward trend might ...

Even major players like Blackstone Group have been buying up tens of thousands of homes, placing them into rental service, and selling derivative securities guaranteed by the rents. Whether that strategy works or not, it's clear that many real estate market analysts expect the demand for rentals to continue to grow. Rents have been steadily increasing in almost every market as well.

Refer back to Chapter 8 for the valuation calculations used to evaluate and select rental properties. When the numbers work, rental home investors enjoy double-digit returns on their investments, and many have retired to their dream location to enjoy life.

If you're considering rental property as a long-term investment, don't shy away just because you don't have the cash to buy homes outright. Actually, it's really not the best approach. Leverage with mortgages provides a much better return on cash invested; the ROI is far better than any savings account or certificate of deposit. If you don't have the cash for a down payment, refer back to the chapter on funding your deals, and you may just find that you are able to partner up with another investor or family member who will invest cash to couple with your investment of expertise in property selection, negotiation, and management.

Obviously, I don't know your financial situation, but to illustrate how wealth is being created through rental property investment, we'll just assume that an investor has $300,000 in savings. This money could be in savings accounts, CDs, a poorly performing stock investment account, or a retirement account than can be switched over to a self-directed IRA or 401k for real estate investment. Even if you're starting with much less cash, using other strategies I've covered can get you some down payment money pretty quickly.

Like many people, this investor may have been settling for an average return across all of their investments of between 3% and 6%. If they're weighted toward safety or insured deposits, it would be at the low end of that range. Let's see what that same $300,000 could return if invested in rental homes.

It's unrealistic to assume you can make a bulk purchase of a half dozen homes that are all at the same price, but we'll do a chart assuming very similar homes of the same price to make this concept easier to illustrate. There's a lot of latitude in how you structure your portfolio. You could choose to buy three homes with almost $100,000 down payment on each (before closing costs), or it could be six homes with a down payment of $50,000 each, or any variation of the above.

You're balancing your cash flow requirements with your available cash, risk tolerance, and plan for managing properties. More homes bring more management involvement. Another VERY important thing to remember is that you always want to buy rental homes below current market value. In this type of investing, it's more than just thinking about locking in equity on the front end. It's very much about getting a higher priced home for a lower investment, which brings higher rents for that price range home. This increases your cash flow for the same cash invested. If you always pay full value money, your cash flow and ROI will be significantly lower.

Another thing to remember is that you're leveraging with mortgages. For our example, we're going to use the purchase of four homes with $70,000 as a down payment on each. The remaining money is used for closing costs. These homes have a current market value of $200,000 each, but we're doing it right and buying at an average 12.5% discount, or $175,000 each. Our rents, however, will be higher for the higher market value homes. We're now leveraged and controlling $800,000 in assets for our $300,000 investment.

We've surveyed the local rental market and found that homes in the $200,000 price range can be rented for an average of $1260/month. We'll be financing at a 4.5% mortgage interest rate for a 30-year loan ($100,000 financed). Taxes and insurance will vary by area and choices of coverage, but we'll do a reasonable estimate for this chart. For simplicity, we're not going to estimate vacancy and credit loss. So our net return after expenses here would be lower by whatever your actual experience or estimate of those costs. However, you may also get a better mortgage rate.

For management, I'm using a percentage that is common in some areas which is 8% of rents collected. If you're doing your own management, this goes into your pocket, so you can adjust the bottom line upward up by that amount. Repairs and maintenance are just estimates.

The purpose of this exercise is to give you a clear picture of the potential return on investment when you use the skills you learn in this book to value, select, purchase and manage rental homes. I'm also going to re-introduce you to the 1031 Tax Deferred Exchange and how it can multiply your returns using Uncle Sam's money.

| Costs/Income Desc. | 4 Rental Homes |
|---|---|
| Income for the year | 4 x $1260 x 12 = $60,480 |
| Mortgage @ 4.5% | $507/month x 12 x 4 = $24,336 |
| Yearly property taxes | $1,500 x 4 = $6,000 |
| Insurance premium | $950 x 4 = $3,800 |
| Management | $1,210 x 4 = $4,840 |
| Yearly Maintenance costs | $520 x 4 = $2,080 |
| | |
| Gross Cash Flow | $19,424 or $1,619/month |
| | |
| Depreciation deduction | $6,364 x 4 = $25,456 |

Let's take a closer look at those numbers, because there's a lot more here, like what's under the surface when you see an iceberg. If you left the $300,000 in investments averaging 5%, your return would be $1250/month. At first glance, it may not seem worth the hassle to manage four rental homes for an extra $369/month. Let's look at the whole story.

- **Expense deductions:**
  - Repair costs
  - Other maintenance costs
  - Management costs
  - Advertising and marketing costs
  - Insurance costs
  - Property taxes
  - Mortgage interest

- **Depreciation** – Most rental real estate can be depreciated over 27.5 years. This is only for the structure, so you value it less the value of the land on which it sits. The number in the chart comes from subtracting $50,000 as land value from the $175,000 purchase price (you can't use the higher true value).

- **What you net** – That $1,250/month from other investments is normally taxed in the year received (ignoring value appreciation, just considering dividends or interest income). At a 25% cumulative tax rate, you're really netting around $1,250 X .75 = $938/month.

- **Don't forget inflation & interest rate risk** – Real estate and rental cash flows are still impacted by inflation, but not as much. You're also locked into your mortgage rate, so interest rate risk isn't a factor like it is when you are selling a bond.

Between the deductions listed and the depreciation deduction, it's possible to have zero tax liability on rental cash flow (consult an accountant). You may even be able to use excess losses to offset other investment income. Suddenly it's not $369/month difference, but more like $681/month or more. Getting better purchase discounts, cutting costs, and raising rents can all increase your ROI.

## Another Approach

We should look at this again, but this time we'll change a few things to give you a better picture of how the numbers come together. This time we'll buy six homes that have retail values of $150,000 each, and we're going to bargain our way to $135,000 purchase prices. Homes valued at $150,000 in this neighborhood rent on average for $1050/month.

We'll put $45,000 down on each, financing $90,000. We're depreciating based on a structure value/cost of $100,000. Let's look at our adjusted chart:

| Costs/Income Desc. | 6 Rental Homes |
|---|---|
| Income for the year | 6 x $1,050 x 12 = $75,600 |
| Mortgage @ 4.5% | $456/month x 12 x 6 = $32,832 |
| Yearly property taxes | $1,100 x 6 = $6,600 |
| Insurance premium | $820 x 6 = $4,920 |
| Management | $1,210 x 6 = $7,260 |
| Yearly Maintenance costs | $480 x 6 = $2,880 |
| | |
| Gross Cash Flow | $21,108 or $1,759/month |
| | |
| Depreciation deduction | $3,636 x 6 = $21,818 |

Comparing these two charts shows the trade-off you make when deciding on price ranges for your investments. Of course, it depends on what's available in your market and how much rents are. In some areas, $135,000 buys as much house as $200,000 in others. But, in this example, it's probably not going to be a good trade-off with only $140/month increase in rents for the management headaches involved with owning another couple of properties.

## Capital Gains Taxes

Other than some kinds of tax-exempt investments or lower return government bonds, you're going to be paying capital gains taxes on gains when assets are sold at a profit. Even when you're depositing funds into IRA or 401k accounts on an after-tax basis, at some point when they're withdrawn you'll be paying taxes.

- The IRS 1031 Tax Deferred Exchange allows you to use even more leverage to grow your portfolio safely. The simple description is that you can roll the profits of the sale of a real estate investment into another like-kind investment and defer capital gains into the future. There are plenty of restrictions and rules:

- There must be an exchange of investment properties, but it doesn't have to be a direct swap of one for the other.

- They must both be held for investment, no personal property or residences.

- They must be like-kind. For our purposes, this is plenty broad. You can use this rule in selling a home and buying land, selling a commercial property and buying rental homes, etc. Like-kind simply means, in our case, real estate.

- The sale and purchase must be an "integrated" transaction, even if they're not happening at the same time. A third independent party (a qualified intermediary) accepts the proceeds of the property sale and then disperses them in the purchase transaction closing. They never pass through the hands of the investor.

- There are other rules and time frames for identifying the replacement property (ies) and completing the transactions.

- There are other rules concerning calculating the "tax basis" in the property, so you should never jump into this without accounting advice.

Choosing a qualified intermediary is very important, as recently there have been instances of financial default of intermediaries and the money of investors lost in the process. It sounds complex, and there are more rules that we haven't even mentioned. But using this strategy can grow your portfolio faster and allow you to exchange properties to move up in value.

## You can take it with you! – Kind of...

As long as you do a qualified exchange every time you sell an investment property, you keep moving your liability to pay capital gains into the future. If you sell one without an exchange, you pay the capital gains at that time.

An investor who goes through their life doing these exchanges properly will avoid capital gains completely. How? At the investor's death, the properties covered are passed to their heirs at the new stepped-up current market value. It's as if an entire life of profits just disappears, but leaves the value for the estate.

### It's a Business

Rental property investment is like any other business in that a large part of your success is understanding your market and controlling costs. Because markets evolve, the calculations that validated a great investment on the front end may not be valid a few years down the road. If things have gone your way, rents may have increased, allowing you to increase your gross rental income. However, this is usually associated with inflationary pressures, so your costs may have gone up as well.

Using the 1031 exchange, you have some latitude in adjusting your portfolio over time. When some neighborhoods seem to be declining and rents aren't rising, you can sell those homes and move to other neighborhoods or better opportunities.

---

### Perspectives & Progress

This chapter may have changed your focus a bit, as there is so much long-term wealth creation possible through rental investing. However, you can be using multiple strategies at the same time in your investment business.

You also should pay attention to the information in the next chapter, as it's not a walk in the park. Property management can help you or hurt you. You're dealing with people, renters, and there are legal and liability issues. Get both sides of the business story before you jump into rental property investment.

*Chapter 21*

---

# Rental Property Management is More than Just Collecting Rent

*"An example of good debt is the debt on the apartment houses I own.*
*That debt is good only as long as there are tenants to pay my mortgages.*
*If tenants stop paying their rent, my good debt turns into bad debt."*
*– Robert Kiyosaki*

Don't you just love the idea of a bunch of houses each generating cash flow every month? That's the first thing that comes to mind when people look into rental property investment, and that's the way it should be. But, just like any business, there are costs and management challenges that have a major influence on that cash flow.

In this chapter we'll look at the two major components of rental property management: legal and logistical. In the legal, you'll get an idea of the areas of concern to keep yourself out of the courtroom. Though laws vary by state, they're similar in many respects when it comes to tenant-landlord relationships and the rights of parties in a lease. For the logistical piece, we'll look at managing maintenance, rent collections, vacancy refits and expense control.

# Rental Property Legal Concerns

Overview of Landlord-Tenant Laws

Knowledge of state law is crucial to both landlords and tenants. Landlords want to run a profitable business and protect their investment. Tenants want to be happy in their rental homes and protect their rights. And both landlords and tenants want to avoid legal hassles when it comes to rent, deposits, repairs, and other key issues. The bottom line is that a successful landlord-tenant relationship depends heavily on both landlords and tenants knowing and complying with dozens of state laws.

| Overview of Landlord-Tenant Laws in Your State | | | |
|---|---|---|---|
| Alabama | Illinois | Montana | Rhode Island |
| Alaska | Indiana | Nebraska | South Carolina |
| Arizona | Iowa | Nevada | South Dakota |
| Arkansas | Kansas | New Hampshire | Tennessee |
| California | Kentucky | New Jersey | Texas |
| Colorado | Louisiana | New Mexico | Utah |
| Connecticut | Maine | New York | Vermont |
| Delaware | Maryland | North Carolina | Virginia |
| D.C. | Massachusetts | North Dakota | Washington |
| Florida | Michigan | Ohio | West Virginia |
| Georgia | Minnesota | Oklahoma | Wisconsin |
| Hawaii | Mississippi | Oregon | Wyoming |
| Idaho | Missouri | Pennsylvania | |

The image is a screenshot from nolo.com, a legal website. As you can see, any thorough discussion of the legal aspects of landlord-tenant relationships requires state-specific information. However, the different states have many legal similarities, and the intent of the laws is to protect both parties and establish their rights in the relationship. These laws do tend to favor tenants in most states. Let's choose a state arbitrarily and look at some of the legal aspects of landlord and tenant relationships.

## *Application and Interview*

In this area you can get into trouble not only at the local and state level, but at the federal level as well. Equal opportunity and other discrimination laws govern what you can ask in a rental application or interview, and these laws even state illegal reasons for denying a lease to a prospective tenant. There's no need to let it scare you away from rental investing, but you do need to cover the bases legally.

- Use a legal application approved by a real estate attorney in your state.

- Write out your questions for the interview and stick to your list. Get your questions approved by an attorney as well, or do thorough research with a reputable legal resource. Don't let idle conversation lead you astray such that you ask a question that's illegal.

One state's landlord tenant law website has these can and can't questions. The landlord CAN ask you questions such as the following:

- What kind of job do you have and how long have you worked there?
- How much money do you earn and how often are you paid?
- How many people will be living in the apartment?
- Have you ever been convicted of a felony?
- Are you a registered sex offender?

The landlord CANNOT ask you about the following:

- Your race, ethnicity, or national origin.
- Your religion or religious beliefs.
- Your sexual orientation or marital status.
- Whether you have children under age 18 living with you.
- Whether you have mental or physical disabilities.

Remember to check your state's laws, as they can add layers to the federal list.

### Rental Deposits

It would be poor business to allow someone to occupy your property without some types of deposits to cover non-payment of rent and damages. As property owners and landlords, the more protection the better, but there are both business and legal limitations on what we require for up-front deposits.

- **First/last month rent in advance:** To try and minimize losses if a tenant needs to be evicted or abandons the property while behind on rent, one common approach is to require the first and last month's rent at move-in. Sometimes this isn't affordable for the cash challenged renter, so if it's legal the landlord can add something to each month's rent for two or three months to get that last month's deposit.

- **Damage deposits:** This is a refundable deposit if there are no damages to the property beyond what is considered "normal wear and tear." This is a term that is too broad unless the lease is clear as to what is considered "normal."
  - Stains on carpets or walls.
  - Wall scratches or scars from furniture.
  - Scratches in floor from moving furniture.
  - Holes in the wall from hanging pictures, etc.

- **Pet deposits:** When legally allowed, these are extra deposits required for keeping pets in the rental. They are often required over and above normal damage deposits.

Technically, the first and last month's rent is not a deposit but rent paid in advance. However, if the tenant pays rent the first of the month for the coming month and moves out before that month is up, there could be a refund due. It's those damage deposits that cause disputes and sometimes create legal problems for landlords. From a state website, the left side of this shot is normal wear/tear, and the right is considered damage that could require deposit withholding:

| Ordinary Wear and Tear: Landlord's Responsibility | Damage or Excessive Filth: Tenant's Responsibility |
|---|---|
| Curtains faded by the sun | Cigarette burns in curtains or carpets |
| Water-stained linoleum by shower | Broken tiles in bathroom |
| Minor marks on or nicks in wall | Large marks on or holes in wall |
| Dents in the wall where a door handle bumped it | Door off its hinges |
| Moderate dirt or spotting on carpet | Rips in carpet or urine stains from pets |
| A few small tack or nail holes in wall | Lots of picture holes or gouges in walls that require patching as well as repainting |
| A rug worn thin by normal use | Stains in rug caused by a leaking fish tank |
| Worn gaskets on refrigerator doors | Broken refrigerator shelf |
| Faded paint on bedroom wall | Water damage on wall from hanging plants |
| Dark patches of ingrained soil on hardwood floors that have lost their finish and have been worn down to bare wood | Water stains on wood floors and windowsills caused by windows being left open during rainstorms |
| Warped cabinet doors that won't close | Sticky cabinets and interiors |
| Stains on old porcelain fixtures that have lost their protective coating | Grime-coated bathtub and toilet |
| Moderately dirty mini-blinds | Missing mini-blinds |
| Bathroom mirror beginning to "de-silver" (black spots) | Mirrors caked with lipstick and makeup |
| Clothes dryer that delivers cold air because the thermostat has given out | Dryer that won't turn at all because it's been over-loaded |
| Toilet flushes inadequately because mineral deposits have clogged the jets | Toilet won't flush properly because it's stopped up with a diaper |

Clarity and detail in the lease is the best line of defense when it comes to damage deposits. Each item that is considered normal wear and tear should be described and even illustrated if necessary. Every item that isn't should be clearly stated as well. If you require that no-hole picture hangers be used, then you would be clear about this in the lease and state that holes for hanging will be considered damage requiring repair payment out of deposits.

### Deposit Refunds

In state law there are normally very specific time periods during which the landlord must refund any deposits that aren't legally being withheld. From Colorado law:

What about when a tenant moves out? What is the deadline in Colorado for returning a security deposit?

Under Colorado law, a landlord must return the tenant's security deposit within one month, unless the lease agreement specifies a longer period of time (which may be no more than 60 days). The landlord must return the deposit within 72 hours (not counting weekends or holidays) if a hazardous condition involving gas equipment required the tenant to leave.

You'll find that though the time frames vary, there will almost always be a deadline by which deposits must be refunded. Get a valid forwarding address and you may want to use certified mail for proof of delivery, though a cancelled check should work as well if they actually do receive the refund.

### Withholding Rent

The Internet makes it easy for renters to research their rights. Though they may not always use an accurate source, tenants are in many cases very educated about their rights in the relationship. It is unfortunate that many tenants enter the relationship with a preconceived idea that landlords need to be policed.

There are specific allowable reasons for not paying rent, and you want to avoid situations that lead to rent interruptions. When you're notified of problems with comfort systems, such as air conditioning or heating not working during weather extremes, jump on getting them repaired. This could be justification of withholding rent, just as plumbing and electrical problems can result in non-payment of rent for the period the problems persist.

### Entry into Unit

There will be some restrictions on entry by the landlord into the residence. In many states 24 hour notice must be given unless an emergency situation exists (such as a gas leak, etc.). There are situations where the 24 hour notice would not apply, such as letting repair people in to the property based on a problem reported by the tenant.

Know the rules, state them clearly in the lease, and abide by them. There is no sense in increasing your vacancy losses because you've unnecessarily annoyed good tenants. As always in a business, it's best to document tenant complaints and requests in writing to cover you in case there is some misunderstanding as to your entry into the residence. Email helps us in this regard. Use that Evernote account to file away email communications with tenants in case you need them in the future.

### *Non-payment of Rent & Eviction*

There is far too much detail and many differences in the laws from state to state to get into too much detail about eviction in this book. However, a few general points can get you started in research and conversations with an attorney to get your lease and rules set up legally for your best interests:

- Exactly when rent is due.
- How and where rent can be paid..
- How many days after the due date rent is considered to be late.
- When they'll receive a notice of late rent.
- When legal action will proceed if they don't pay within an acceptable and defined period.
- How eviction notice is served and when.
- What constitutes abandonment of the property and what happens to any personal property left in the residence?
- What happens to deposits in an eviction?

There is no more painful procedure than an eviction process, so you don't want to complicate it by doing things wrong or missing deadlines and notice requirements.

These aren't all of the legal factors in rental property investment, but they're some of the most important. I'm not trying to scare you away, because we can hire professionals such as an attorney to a full management firm to help us out.

### The Logistics of Rental Property Management

You're running a business for profit, and in every line item involved in management of your properties you have responsibilities and opportunities. This is a good thing, as you have far more control over your profitability in rental property investing than in the stock market. You're not just the owner of the asset, you're the manager. If you can improve on your management process and cut your costs while maintaining quality, you'll dramatically improve your ROI.

### Rents and Marketing

We've gone through rental market research and setting rents to be profitable yet competitive. This is an ongoing process, as markets are constantly changing. Definitely study the market and re-evaluate your rents 30 or so days before lease expirations, as you may need to adjust for the next tenant or lease renewal.

Marketing can be as simple as a classified ad, a *Craigslist* ad, or website or social media advertising. Listing on homes for rent sites can be effective, though there will be a cost there as well.

The screenshot of the home page of *ForRentByOwner.com* is an example of a site to get some extensive online exposure for your rental. Notice that they get it placed on *Zillow.com* and *Trulia.com* as well.

If you decide to hire a management company, they'll have established advertising arrangements, as well as possible discounts for long-term ad placement in local newspapers or other print media. In some markets, rental advertising can be free and as simple as a card on a college or business bulletin board.

### Rent Collection

We're mostly engaged in single family rental homes, and our properties can be spread all over town. You don't want to be knocking on doors to collect rent. Your lease should be specific as to due dates (when you receive, not when they mail), and the address where you want the rent received. Here is what has been common:

- **Collecting rent in cash:** While this may seem a great solution, as cash in hand is always comforting, you must somehow meet up with your tenant to make this work. And you need to write them a receipt.

- **Check payment of rent:** Mailing checks is the most common rent collection method. It works as long as the checks are good. If a check bounces, you incur fees, and you then need to recoup them from a tenant already having a problem with rent payment.

- **Money orders:** This can be more reassuring for you as a landlord, but it's inconvenient for your tenant.

### Direct Bank Deposit

The digital age brings us improved methods for many things, and collecting rent is one. Most banks will now help you set up electronic transfers from your tenants' bank accounts to yours on the day when the rent is due. It's usually as easy as getting them to sign the bank's form and keep money in the bank. This works well because you're already maintaining an account for rents, or you should be as a separate entity for IRS purposes.

### Debit and Credit Cards

You'll find that many management companies are already allowing rent payments via credit and debit cards. The good news is that payments are instantly verified, and the money is yours immediately or within 24 hours.

The other side is the fees you'll pay. You don't have to get one of those credit card swiping machines with a monthly fee. You can set up a PayPal account and simply bill them for rent online via email or a website payment button and have them pay online as well. At this time, PayPal charges $0.30 per transaction plus a fee that varies between 1.9% and 2.9% of the amount processed. This can get expensive over a year of rents. You may want to reserve this method of payment for tenants who seem to have a problem or have a temporary shortfall, offering it when necessary.

### Utilities

Owners leasing units out for 6 months or a year or longer generally require that tenants pay utilities, at least electric, gas and Internet. Trash and water are often paid by the landlord. Some lower-priced rental units are rented out with "utilities included," but they're generally smaller and there's not a lot of opportunity to run up bills when there are only minimal appliances and small spaces to heat and cool.

As many of the sewer and water services are supplied by the municipality, non-payment of these fees can result in a lien on the property, so landlords generally like to control these payments. The electric and gas companies can cut off service, but they usually can't create a lien on the home.

### Repairs

Repairs are fixing things broken or not working properly. This includes appliances, heating, cooling, broken windows, damages to counters, floors, walls, etc. They are normally deductible in the year in which they are incurred. As you own more homes, you can often negotiate discounted services from repair contractors, but balance that with response time.

You don't want tenant problems or lost revenue because repairs are delayed or drawn out. Keeping a tenant for a couple of years can be far more valuable to you than saving $50 on a plumbing repair. Set up relationships with repair people so you aren't thumbing through the yellow pages when you need someone in the moment. When they respond and perform promptly, pay them promptly and you'll get them quickly the next time you need them. Also, ask them to let you know of any odd situations or damage they may see when in the home.

### Renovation

Renovation is different from repair, in that it is usually a capital improvement, not deductible in the year in which you pay for it. It is depreciated. You may not need to do any renovations, but you may find that you can increase the value and rent you can charge if you improve a home's appearance or add a room/bedroom/bath.

Renovations should be part of a long-term budgeting plan for a property, and you should know in advance what you will likely want to do. Talk to an accountant if large repairs crop up unexpectedly, such as roof replacement. Straight from the IRS website:

Depreciation & Recapture

**Question:** We have incurred substantial repairs to our residential rental property: new roof, gutters, windows, furnace, and outside paint. What are the IRS rules concerning depreciation?

**Answer:**
**Replacements** of roof, rain gutters, windows and furnace on a residential rental property:
* Are capital improvements to the property because they are for betterments and/or restorations to the property.
* Would be in the same class of property as the residential rental property to which they are attached.
* Are generally depreciated over a recovery period of 27.5 years using the straight line method of depreciation and a mid-month convention since the property is residential rental property.

**Repairs**, such as repainting the residential rental property:
* Are generally currently deductible expenses.
* Do not improve the property, but keep your property in an ordinarily efficient operating condition.

**Note:** Repainting your property, fixing gutters or floors, fixing leaks, plastering, and replacing broken windows are examples of repairs. If you make repairs as part of an extensive remodeling or restoration of your property and these repairs directly benefit or are incurred due to this restoration of your property, then the whole job is a capital improvement. In that case, you should capitalize and depreciate the repair costs as the same class of property that you have restored or remodeled as discussed above.

### Insurance

Insurance is an expense over which you have some control. You'll obviously need liability to protect yourself from your tenants, but you can choose options when it comes to the structure itself. There are different levels of coverage, from full replacement on down, and you definitely can cut your costs by increasing deductibles.

For insurance you should work with an independent agent who can shop your needs with multiple insurers. It can make a major difference in your cost and give you more options. Building a relationship with a great insurance broker can save you a lot of money over time, and it can help you to evaluate purchases with insurance estimates before you buy.

### Liability and Safety

Your rental homes should have good door and window locks for your security as well as that of your tenants. A security system is valuable, and your tenants will appreciate it. You should also factor in the amount needed to have the locks changed between tenants, at the very least if they're in the home for a year or more. You have no idea who they may have given a key to.

Have quality smoke detectors installed and keep them serviced. If the home has gas or propane heating, have a $CO_2$ detector as well. As mentioned earlier in the book, your notice that you need access every six months to change the batteries will be welcomed by the tenants and give you a chance to inspect the property.

### It's Your Investment

Proper management of your properties will protect your investment, increase your ROI, and keep them in a condition that will increase your selling price on the other end. The trade-off can be a build-up of a tired and/or bad attitude over time. In the next chapter, we'll talk about hiring professional management.

## Perspectives & Progress

Before you invest in your first rental property, it's time to think about future management. You can decide if you want to manage on your own until you reach a specific number of properties. Start looking into management companies, repair vendors, and others who will be a part of your support system.

Think about budgeting and how you'll handle expenses, rent collection, and banking. If you're considering accepting debit and credit cards, start a PayPal account and try to estimate how many of your rent transactions will go that way. In other words, you don't have to add 2.9% to all of your rents if you're not taking cards for every month's payments.

---

### Chapter 22

# *Outsourcing Property Management*

*"The success combination in business is: Do what you do better...*
*and: do more of what you do...." – David Joseph Schwartz*

The quote above is really important for the real estate rental property investor who wants to replicate their success and grow their business. If your goal is one to four or so rental homes, you can probably enjoy life and retirement while handling your management duties.

However, if you don't like dealing with tenants, or you want to add to your portfolio and build on your success, outsourcing property management is the way to go. You're still the owner of your business, and you will want to manage for success. But, managing for success includes knowing when and how to delegate responsibility and tasks so you can focus on growth or just enjoying life.

## Why Outsource Your Property Management?

There are always reasons for keeping control and not hiring out any of your property management duties. Usually we just believe that nobody else will care as much about our business as we do, so they won't do as good a job. Let's look at arguments for letting go of some of the tasks involved in property management.

### *Your Time*

All of the other tasks and activities we talk about here require someone's time. Right now it's your time that is invested in communicating with tenants, marketing, advertising, supervising repairs, and more. As you are approach retirement, you have to ask yourself if handling tenant complaints is one of the things you want to do with your time.

### *Quality is a Concern*

Any way you look at it, as you add properties your management becomes a part-time activity that can take the place of having fun or enjoying retirement. A property management company does these things for a living. Their business depends on doing it right. Their business grows and prospers if they provide quality service.

### *Legal Issues*

Specializing in property management requires a focus on the legal aspects to protect the management business. Landlord/tenant law is complicated and requires constant monitoring of changes in regulations and new laws. There are many ways to get in trouble with tenant relationships, and a company specializing in this area should keep you out of court.

### *Profits*

Though contracting for property management costs money, you will see a return on your investment over time. Closer scrutiny of your properties, regular preventive maintenance, faster and more efficient rent collection, and other activities that improve and enhance your properties will increase your ultimate profits.

## Choosing the Company

Whether you are hiring a one-person show, a new small management company, or a large established property management firm, you need to know certain things about the company and how they do business.

### Reporting to You

You want to ask about their reporting to property owners. At the very least, you'll want monthly reports about your properties, probably coinciding with the deposits of your rent proceeds less their fees. These reports should let you know of any condition or repair issues, as well as any new current market information that may influence rents.

### Property Inspections

You want to know how often and when the management company will enter the property to inspect for problems and condition. You don't want to pay extra for inspections.

### How do they Charge?

What is their fee structure? You want their fees based on actual rent collected, not potential rents. If they don't collect from a tenant, you don't want to be paying them a percentage of what they never received. Get a schedule of charges for extra services not included with their normal fees.

### How do they Fill Vacancies?

What do they do for marketing and advertising? What are their interview procedures and how do they check out references and ability to pay rent? What are their paperwork and legal procedures to properly vet prospective tenants?

### Maintenance Procedures and Cost Handling

Take a look at their contracted list of vendors for repairs and maintenance. Are they reputable companies with good references, or do they work only with low bidders? What are the management company's procedures when a tenant calls in a repair issue? How do they pay contractors, and do they have negotiated discounts to save you money? How do they report expenditures to you, and at what dollar amounts must they agree to get your approval before taking action?

### Their Financials

In many states property management companies are required to have escrow accounts for handling all client business. All funds must be separated from other funds and accounts of the ownership and management of the company. Even if not required, you want to be sure that the management company is financially sound and operates with proper scrutiny and financial reporting.

### Their Leases

Read one of their leases. If you have any concerns, run it by your attorney. Who is their attorney? The lease document and your contract with the management company are crucial, so get whatever advice you need to reach a comfort level necessary for a long-term relationship.

## The Ultimate Business Model

It wouldn't be a thorough treatment of the rental property management topic without considering growth to a level that creates another opportunity. Some very successful investors reach a point where they see a chance to leverage their profits by hiring themselves as property managers.

The idea is to start a property management company totally separate from the rental investment business. This company, usually a LLC or other corporate entity, is then hired to manage the investment company's properties. The fees paid are deductible to the rental property investment company. The property management company runs like any business, with income and expenses, and separate tax liability.

This is only for the investment business that has grown to a level where a separate profitable and integrated business is a logical next step. First, you move from total control, then through out-sourcing, and finally back to control with a whole new and separate profit center.

---

## Perspectives & Progress

It's never too early to start checking out property managers. You may not need them for a year or more, but when you're ready, it's going to be an easier process to get moving if you've been doing your research along the way.

*Chapter 23*

# Lease-To-Own &
# The Profitable Sandwich

*"I sold my house this week. I got a pretty good price for it, but it made my landlord mad as hell." – Gary Shandling*

Gary Shandling's joke is funny, but it also leads us into this chapter. We will discuss a couple of investment strategies in using lease-to-own, otherwise known as rent-to-own or lease-purchase. We're going to take a detailed look at two specific lease-purchase deals for investment profits:

1. Acquiring a property through lease-purchase.
2. Leasing that property to a tenant buyer through a second lease-purchase.

This is sometimes called a "sandwich lease," so our photo is certainly showing where the cash flow is: in the middle.

The overall goal of this type of investing is to locate a motivated seller and lease their property with an option to buy on or before a specified date in the future. We then work with a tenant buyer who isn't able to purchase in the present, but wants to purchase in the future. We put them in the home on a lease with option to buy, but at a cash flow profit each month. Let's look at it in detail, building our sandwich with our profit in the middle.

## Lease-purchase of a Home

We're marketing for motivated sellers who aren't able to sell in the current market. Perhaps there is just poor buyer activity, or maybe they are unable to get a price that will cover their closing costs and real estate commissions. They may need to relocate for a job, and they have no desire to become a landlord.

### *Marketing for the Sandwich Lease Strategy*

In our marketing chapter, we discussed how to market for both buyers and sellers, building a buyer list and searching for sellers with properties our buyers will purchase. Much of the emphasis is usually on wholesaling and flipping to rental investors, but now we have a different target market.

Our newspaper ads, Craigslist ads, websites, social media posts, and bandit signs are focused on finding people who would like to buy a home but aren't able to right now. Usually it's poor credit history, lack of a down payment, or both. They're renting but would really like to own.

> *"Bad credit? You can still buy a home. We can help."*
> *"Buy a home with low/no down payment. We have homes."*
> *"Rent to Own Your New Home"*

As we discussed in the marketing chapter, you should run ads with homes for lease with popular features in popular neighborhoods like:

> *"3 BR, 2 BA home in popular Barstow neighborhood for lease-to-own. Poor credit, no down payment, no problem."*

These types of ads will begin to build a buyer list of people who want to own but thought they couldn't. Just tell them the home you advertised is taken, but you'll find them one that meets their desires. Get their requirements, where they'd like to live, and then match homes you find with the buyers who really want them.

## Helping Sellers Move

Let's get one thing out of the way right away. If these people could sell, they would have done so by the time you reach them. They have one or more problems that have kept them in their homes when they want to move. You can provide a valuable service to them, and it's usually going to be happily accepted once you explain how it works.

You're going to help them move on to their new home or job location, and even provide a little money for them to use in the move. Even if they owe about what their home is worth, you may be able to help them. Of course you will run the numbers to make sure you can make the deal work before you make promises or offers. Here is what you need to determine to make sure that the deal will work for you:

1. The value of the home in the current market and the balance due on the mortgage.

2. That there are no other liens or mortgages on the property.

3. What you can charge for rent in the current market.

4. That the rent you charge less the amount of their mortgage payment will create acceptable positive cash flow.

5. That they will let you lease the home for the amount of their payment with taxes and insurance escrowed.

6. If they're behind on payments, that you can work out a way to catch them up and still make the deal work.

7. You can make a profit on the sale of the home in the future after paying off the mortgage.

If all of these requirements are met, you will attempt to contract with them to lease their home for the amount of their monthly mortgage payment with an option to buy between one and five years in the future. You will negotiate your purchase price to work with your future expected value and selling price for a profit on the other end. Let's go through an example deal to see how it works.

### The home and seller:

The home is a 3BR, 2BA home with an attached garage in a popular neighborhood you know will be liked by one or more tenant-buyers on your list. They have a 30-year mortgage with a low interest rate and a payment of $785/month with taxes and insurance escrowed. There are no other liens or mortgages on the property. It is currently valued at $167,000, which is lower than when they bought it, and they owe $165,500 on their mortgage.

You offer to lease their property for the amount of their payment, $785/month knowing that you can rent it out for $1090/month. That's a positive cash flow of $305/month. You use a three year lease with an option to purchase the home at the end of the lease for $168,000. A mortgage amortization table shows that regular payments for three years would result in a mortgage payoff of $157,000. Your estimate of the value of the home in three years with conservative appreciation is $188,000.

Here's how your numbers look if all of your estimates and actual payments work through to a purchase/sale in three years:

- $305/month x 36 months = $10,980 cash flow profits
- $31,000 profit at sale less closing costs.

You've tried to be conservative in your estimates, so you expect to do better. The most important thing to remember is that you have the right, not the obligation, to buy the home in the future. You'll enjoy the positive cash flow throughout the deal as long as you can keep it occupied by a tenant.

### The option premium:

You're going to have to pay the seller a premium for the option to buy, and it will be cash when the lease-purchase is finalized. Let's say that in our example you agree to $3,500. They get this money to help with their move, but don't worry because you're going to get it back from your tenant buyer, and you may possibly get even more. Next we'll look at the other side of our sandwich and how we work with the tenant buyer on the other end.

## The Other Side of the Sandwich – Helping a Tenant to Buy

Remember that we have been building our tenant buyer list through marketing, and we know that we have at least one buyer who will love this home. In fact, before we signed the lease-purchase with the seller, we either showed detailed photos to our tenant-buyer or, preferably, visited the home with them. We even negotiated our deal and prepared a lease-purchase agreement to be immediately signed when we lock up the property.

Our tenant buyer has agreed to our rent of $1,090/month, and we've prepared our lease-purchase with an option for them to buy on or before the lease expiration date three years in the future. They have agreed to pay fair market value or $188,000, whichever is greater at the time they purchase. They now have time to work on improving their credit score and saving up for their down payment.

In return for the option to buy, they agree to pay an option premium of $4,000. You immediately pocket the $500 difference, and they have the home they want to own locked up for far less than they would have needed for a down payment.

## Added Benefits

This isn't a typical tenant-landlord relationship. These people intend to own this home. They are benefitting from having it under their control for three years with a contract to purchase at any time up until lease expiration. That's their benefit, but you are doing well also.

They're going to treat the home better because they want to own it in good condition. You can often even negotiate for them to take care of some repairs, especially normal wear and tear. You can even negotiate larger repairs on a shared basis in some cases. As a landlord, you have a resident caretaker and will have lower repair costs over time. They may even make some improvements at their expense. Your taxes and insurance are paid out of the mortgage escrow, so surprises are doubtful.

## What if the Plan Goes Wrong?

Let's say that you're rocking along a year or so after you pull this deal together and the tenant-buyer decides to bail on you. They have financial problems or perhaps are transferred to another state for work. You get to keep their $4,000 option deposit; the seller also gets to keep your $3,500 deposit. All isn't lost, though.

It's still your home to rent out, and you've been adding to your buyer list all along. It's probable that you can call a few people on your list and get another tenant into the property very quickly. Remember that your tenant-buyer is breaking a lease, so you have some recourse to recoup lost rent from them if they have any money. The worst case, if this is your approach, would be the loss of a month's rent and cash flow if you replace them with a new tenant and they can't pay you for the lost rent. But there is a possible silver lining in this cloud.

If you can place another tenant-buyer in the home, you can collect another non-refundable option premium deposit. This is added profit, and you also get a second chance to look at value appreciation and rent amounts. You may be able to negotiate a higher selling price on the other end, and you may be able to raise the rent.

The only issue is that you can't take this new lease past your original three year end date on the first one unless you extend that agreement with the original seller, or can buy them out when that lease-purchase expires.

Of course, you can also just place a regular tenant into the home without any option to buy. You just continue to rent the home out until your original lease with the seller runs to conclusion. You then can either just walk away without obligation, or you can possibly flip the home to a rental investor if the numbers work.

## The Sandwich Lease is Complex, but it Works

There are a number of steps and contractual negotiations involved in this investment strategy, but they're usually well worth it. You do need to do several due diligence tasks before you try this investment strategy:

- Make sure it's legal where you live.
- Get your attorney to write or approve your lease-purchase agreements.
- Diligently build as large of a buyer list as possible. Good deals are only good if you have buyers to pick up your obligations at a profit.

This strategy works very well for those who want to be rental property investors with minimal cash invested.

---

### Perspectives & Progress

This isn't an investment strategy for everyone, but you may want to take some time to survey your market for opportunities. Running some test ads on Craigslist for tenant buyers can give you an idea of the potential. Running ads at the same time for motivated sellers might even yield some immediate possible deals for you.

### Chapter 24

# *More Niche Strategies:*
# *Profit Outside the Mainstream*

*"The ability to perceive or think differently is more important than the knowledge gained." – David Bohm*

In sales and management meetings, companies like to tell their employees to "think outside of the box," meaning be inventive and think of different solutions to common problems. This chapter is a little bit of thinking outside the box in real estate investment. These are strategies out of the mainstream, but they can be very profitable.

## Buying Debt

If you're not in the mood to deal with tenants, their calls for clogged toilets, and other rental property-related issues, you can buy mortgage notes. This can be a very profitable niche, but you'll need to learn the ropes so you don't get stuck with non-performing and hard to sell assets.

### Why Mortgage Notes?

As an alternative to property ownership, investors with cash can purchase mortgage notes, lock in returns that they can count on, and minimize their risk with careful due diligence. You don't even have to buy full notes, as you can purchase specified months of return as partial full note investments. Let's see how it works.

### Who Sells Notes?

Many people only think of large lenders and banks when they think of mortgages and notes. But there are many private mortgages out there and more new ones steadily coming to market. Private sellers often take back a mortgage and provide seller financing to a buyer. Sometimes it's because the buyer can't qualify for a regular loan, and that isn't always because they're a credit risk. Since the mortgage crash, many lenders are difficult to deal with if the borrower is self-employed. These people often buy with seller financing.

More property owners are financing purchases because the returns on their savings are very low. They can charge a little above regular mortgage interest rates and enjoy better cash flow. This works really well for retirees who have high equity or paid-off mortgages. They can do far better financing their sale for the buyer than getting cash and putting it into the bank.

Some of these note holders will later have a need for cash, and they'll be willing to sell an entire note or a portion to generate immediate cash. One example is a retired person holding a note on a home they sold, but they want to pay off their credit card debt. They can sell a portion of their note to an investor for the cash they need.

### *An example note:*

A self-employed buyer wants to purchase a home for $200,000, but they're a little short of a 20% down payment. They have $35,000 and strong credit and income, so the seller who owns the home outright decides to finance it for them. A higher than current market interest rate of 9% is offered and accepted for a 30 year mortgage. Payments are $1,327.63/month.

Four years into the mortgage all payments have been made on time. Here's the amortization and amount still owed of $159,815.81.

| Aug. 2018 | $ 1,327.63 | $ 127.10 | $ 1,200.53 | $ 57,342.34 | $ 159,943.86 |
| Sept. 2018 | $ 1,327.63 | $ 128.05 | $ 1,199.58 | $ 58,541.92 | $ 159,815.81 |
| Oct. 2018 | $ 1,327.63 | $ 129.01 | $ 1,198.62 | $ 59,740.54 | $ 159,686.80 |

The note holder needs some cash for unexpected medical bills, and a note investor offers to buy all or a part of this note. Forty-eight payments have been made, with 312 left. The investor will buy the note, but at a discount, as today's dollars are worth more than future dollars. The investor offers the note holder $149,000 for the entire note.

Remember that this property is worth at least $200,000, though probably more like $220,000 with four years of appreciation. This means that the $149,000 is 68% LTV (loan to value), which is a nice equity built into the deal. The other benefit is that the investor is getting that same $1,327.63 monthly payment which now represents an annual return of 10.7%.

### *What if the borrower defaults?*

The investor owns the note and has the right to foreclose if the borrower defaults on payments. Then the investor can sell the home on the open market at full value less commissions and costs, or they can flip it to another investor. They can also opt to hold the home and place a tenant in it for rental cash flow.

Basically, the investor enjoys a higher-than-market interest rate return fully guaranteed by real estate. In this example, there is significant property market value over the invested amount, so it's pretty certain that even in a foreclosure there will be some profit in the resale.

In this example, the investor could have purchased just a portion of the note, either by getting a portion of each payment or by buying specific months. An example would be buying the next 36 months for a specified lower investment amount and getting the entire payments for that time period. At the end of the period, the note would revert back to the seller.

### Finding Notes

2 Year Seasoned performing note!!!!        $14,500.00

Unpaid Principal Balance: 17,439.69

Est. Property Value: 35,000

Property Valuation Date: 06/2014

Address: Register Here

Property City: Cumberland

State: Maryland

Property Zip Code: 21052

Original Balance: 20000

Interest Rate: 6

Balloon Pmt: No

Amortization: 10

Note Payment: 222.04

Last Payment Amount: 222.04

Last Payment Date: 6/5/2014

Origination Date: 06/28/2012

Maturity Date: 06/28/2022

Deliquent Taxes: NO

Note Position: 1st

Owner Occupied Property: Yes

Property Type: Single Family

Listed: July 3, 2014 7:32 am

Expires: 11 days

You can start watching different publications and ads for note-buying opportunities, including online searches,. One site found quickly in a Google search is NoteMarketPlace.com. I haven't investigated this site, but the ad above tells us two things. There are online resources for buying notes, and we can see that they come in all types and sizes.

## Tax Liens and Certificates

One estimate is that between $7 billion and $10 billion in property taxes go delinquent each year. Local county and state governments are struggling with their budgets, and delinquent property taxes make the situation worse. In many states they turn to investors for help.

In most states, when a property owner becomes delinquent in payment of their property taxes, the county or state places a lien on the property for the back taxes due. Once this lien is in place, the property can't be sold. Depending on the taxing jurisdiction, interest rates on overdue taxes can run anywhere from 5% to 36%. Examples on high and low ends:

- Kansas 5%
- Oregon 5%
- Oklahoma 8%
- Illinois 36%
- Iowa 24%
- Georgia 20%

There are various ways in which the taxing authorities offer these properties to investors, so check your area. But one common method is to auction them to the bidder willing to take the lowest interest amount. An example would be Florida with an 18%

maximum interest amount. Bidders start there and go downward and the bidder willing to accept the lowest rate wins.

So if a property owner owes $5,000 in back taxes in Florida, bidders may come in at various interest rates, but if the lowest a bidder is willing to accept is 11.5%, then that's the rate they'll get on their immediate $5,000 investment.

In every state there is a period during which the property owner can redeem their property rights by paying the past due taxes, interest, and penalties. Estimates are that between 95% and 99% of all tax liens are paid off rather than losing the property. If the lien isn't paid off within the legal time limit, the lienholder investor can file foreclosure and take possession of the property.

Of course, there are some very important due diligence items involved to make sure you have a reasonably safe and profitable investment:

1.  **What is the property worth?** – You don't want to buy a tax lien on a worthless property. There is little chance the owner will pay the back taxes and interest, and you'll end up with a property you can't sell for what you have invested.

2.  **Ratio of investment to value** – You want to control the highest value for the lowest investment possible. If you can pay $4,500 for a tax lien on a $300,000 property with a low first mortgage, you are likely to see the owner pay up and get your investment back with a nice rate of interest. In the unlikely event that they let you foreclose, you're going to be able to sell at a profit.

Here's an example screenshot from the Illinois online tax sale catalog:

Tax lien investing has become very competitive due to the high rates of return. In some cases the bidders bid down the rates to very low levels. One example would be if taxes are charged quarterly, and bidders get to go back to maximum interest rate for future quarters. An example would be buying the lien with a very low bid, even down to zero percent to get control of it. Then when the owner doesn't pay and future quarters yield a maximum example rate of 18%, the numbers can work out well.

By finding properties worth far more than the taxes owed, you're dramatically reducing your risk. The owner is far more likely to pay the interest and taxes to keep ownership. But if they don't, you're much more likely to be able to sell at a profit after foreclosure.

The rules and time frames can be complicated, so be sure to understand them before bidding for tax liens. The lure for many is that you can start with as little as a few hundred dollars. If you don't have enough for what you know is a good deal, ask friends and family to get involved. They'll be interested in taking a few hundred or thousand dollars out of a savings account yielding 2% to get a real estate secured double-digit return.

This is just an introduction, so you'll need to become much more educated in the process and risks in your tax jurisdiction.

---

### Perspectives & Progress

If you aren't yet ready for rental property ownership and investment, you may want to look into the alternatives in this chapter. If you have the cash, mortgage notes may be your target for investigation. If you're cash challenged, look into tax lien and certificate sales in your market area.

The more you learn, the more choices you'll have to get started in real estate investment very quickly. After reading this chapter and others on wholesaling and bird dogging, even those who are not sitting on much cash can find a way to start generating profits quickly.

---

### Chapter 25

# *You're at the Starting Line.*
# *Hit the Accelerator*

*"I think fearless is having fears but jumping anyway." – Taylor Swift*

You can't cross the finish line if you never start. Jumping in and doing something, even if it's a small start, is what you must do to gain momentum and reach your goals. The great news is that what you learn in this book is not just a strategy for profits in real estate investment. You learn a whole range of strategies, and one or more of them will work for you NOW!

Let's do an overview and review of what you've learned to refresh your memory. This will lead you back to the areas where you want to do more research and gather resources to jump right into a profitable real estate investment business.

## *Chapter 1*

You can do this. You don't need to have been born with a special skill to do it, and everything you need can be learned. This book provides both the training and mindset you need for success.

### Chapter 2

There are very solid reasons for re-allocation of assets from stocks and bonds to real estate. You learned the comparative risk profiles and why real estate is a more secure investment, as well as some amazing tax benefits available only to real estate investors.

### Chapters 3 and 4

In these chapters we did some self-assessment in several areas. How much time do we have to get started in our business, and how can we fit it into our lifestyle and other obligations? What do we have for cash or other investable assets, and what is our attitude about risk in investing? We talked about starting with a plan for investing, setting goals, and adapting to market and life changes along the way.

### Chapter 5

This chapter was all about a tool/resource for our business. We'll be gathering a LOT of data, taking a lot of photos, and checking out information in many locations, including courthouse records. Evernote is free for many functions, but carries a cost for enhanced features. You learned how it works, and how you can use it to gather a lot of information from many sources, file that information from any location, and find it again when you need it. It's the Swiss Army Knife of information storage and retrieval.

### Chapter 6

This chapter is all about market research and becoming an expert for higher profit margins. You can't buy and sell real estate in a vacuum. There are local and national forces influencing prices in your market, and you learned how to keep up with current market data, from local to national, helping you to make wise investment decisions.

### Chapter 7

You're going to be buying and selling real estate, no matter which of the strategies you choose to use most. To do this, you'll need buyers and sellers as your customers. In this very important chapter you learned how you can market to build a strong buyer list, as well as how to locate motivated sellers.

### Chapter 8

This is the numbers chapter. You may only use a few of the valuation and cost calculations here, but they'll be important. Even if you rely on a trusted real estate agent, accountant, or other person to do investment calculations, you need to know how they're done and you need to check on them every now and then.

### Chapter 9

This is the chapter on CMA, Comparative Market Analysis. You'll need to know how this is done, as you always want to know the current market value of a home you own or are considering buying. You'll never want to pay that much, but you do want to know what you're getting for a discount to value. Using this and sharp negotiation skills, you'll be making higher wholesaling profits, as well as increasing your rental cash flow and ROI.

### Chapter 10

The great thing about real estate investment as a business is that you can choose to keep your overhead down to almost nothing. This chapter discusses what you need for this business, and at the entry level it's pretty much stuff you already have. However, it is a business, and knowing your costs and maintaining control are necessary goals.

### Chapter 11

Outsourcing is the subject of this chapter, and you'll definitely need certain professionals on your team from the very beginning.

An Accountant and an attorney are important team members, as you'll be signing leases, purchase agreements, and other legal documents right away. In this chapter we look at building out your investment team as you need them and how to build a team focused on your goals and profit objectives.

### Chapter 12

Every successful business got there by bringing value to their customers. Added value when you're in a chain of transactions is what you must bring to the table if you want to be successful at real estate investment. This chapter presents the value you add to each of the coming strategies in the rest of the book. Knowing what your customers will value is the path to success.

### Chapter 13

Foreclosure properties are candidates for almost every strategy we deal with in our business. This chapter explains the two types of foreclosure, judicial and non-judicial, and how the process works. You also get some resources to locate foreclosure properties.

### Chapter 14

Short sales as an investing niche has evolved since the market crash beginning in 2006. This chapter takes you through that evolution and explains how the banks and lenders have changed their short sale process to encourage more short sale activity. You learn how to help a homeowner and yourself to get through the short sale process to the closing table.

### Chapter 15

An introductory niche for many novice investors is the bird dog role. There are levels of involvement in bird dogging, and this chapter gives you the differences and how they influence the money you make. If you want to get your feet wet with no cash invested, this is a chapter to read again.

### Chapter 16

Wholesaling is the topic of this chapter, and it's a niche that adapts well to any market, up, down, or sideways. It's also a niche that adapts to your financial situation. You have flexibility in how you wholesale using assignment contracts or back-to-back closings. With one you may need very little cash and no financing. With the other you'll make more in profit, but you'll need short-term transaction funding.

### Chapter 17

This is an important chapter to review because financing your deals will become a major factor in your profitability. Growing your business with intelligent financing lowers your risk and gives you flexibility in the deals you can do and the profits you can bank. Read this one again to be sure that you tap every resource available for funding.

### Chapters 18 and 19

These are fun chapters for me, as they're giving you really valuable information about something I love to do: fix & flip. You do more in this niche, but this is also adding more value, so the profits go up as well. If you are interested in fix & flip, go through these chapters again carefully, as you'll want to use the knowledge and resources to lower your risk and increase your profits.

### Chapters 20, 21 and 22

When you see a retiree enjoying a comfortable lifestyle without worries about outspending their income stream, you're probably looking at a real estate investor. They've grown a portfolio of rental properties all generating positive cash flow every month. Learn how to do rental property investing right in these chapters.

### Chapter 23

This chapter may be your introduction to an investment niche used by few in this business, lease-to-own and sandwich leases. It may or may not be a good strategy in your area, but you won't know unless you check it out and apply what you learn in the chapter to market research and some free test marketing. If it will work, it's a way to build rental property cash flow with little or no money out of your pocket.

### *Chapter 24*

Up until sandwich leases, you've learned about the most popular and widely-used real estate investment strategies. Sandwich leases started to move you outside the box in your thinking, and this chapter gets you completely out of the box of traditional real estate investment. Learn about investing in mortgage notes and tax liens, and you just may find these "out of the box" strategies to be real opportunities in your area.

## So you're at the starting line. Now what?

You're sitting at the starting line of your real estate investment business. Good news: you choose your vehicle and how fast you start for the first stage of your business.

You can jam on the race car accelerator and scream down the track, or you can crank the Model T engine and take a slower approach. Either is the right way if it fits your business plan and current time and cash availability.

One of the greatest things about real estate investment as a business is that you can start out slowly and ramp up as you build on past successes. You can start with no cash and no overhead, or you can move some assets around and use them to speed up your business growth.

Whether you crank your business engine with a hand crank or start it with a key in the ignition, the only requirement at this point is to do something. "Start your engine," and move down the track!

**NOTES**

# NOTES

# NOTES